MAX CO

IT'S DOING MY HEAD IN

First Published 2018

by John Catt Educational Ltd,
12 Deben Mill Business Centre, Old Maltings Approach,
Melton, Woodbridge IP12 1BL

Tel: +44 (0) 1394 389850 Fax: +44 (0) 1394 386893
Email: enquiries@johncatt.com
Website: www.johncatt.com

ISBN: 978 1 911382 55 3

Set and designed by John Catt Educational Limited

REVIEWS

It's Doing My Head In *is a must-read for school leaders and aspirers. It is an explosion of theories and models of how harrowed humans cope with the vagaries of educational leadership. When the dust settles, one is captivated by personal stories showing how the theories play out in practice. There is a forensic examination of ways to deal with difficulties, and acknowledgement of the mysteries of Machiavellian minds. Analysis shows the importance of grasping the multi-cultures in which leaders function and the creative ways of bringing mental equilibrium. School problems are the tart of lemons but honey (strategy) adds an antidote for sweet solutions. If you are wanting to understand school communities and how to manage them, through increased self-awareness, consult this book. There is much to reflect upon to enrich knowledge and expertise. Max writes vividly, powerfully and pleasurably.*

Dr Rosemary Sage, Professor of Doctoral Study
School of Education, University of Buckingham

*Max Coates's erudite but immensely readable
book on leadership is unlike any other.*

*Max explores, with humanity, the destructive nature of stress and
shows us how failure to understand its genesis will wreak havoc
on the life of a leader – both professionally and personally.*

*This is a personal take on leadership; yet it is also packed with
masses of scholarly references to prompt further reading and
research for the curious reader. Thoroughly recommended.*

*Anyone who leads, or who aspires to lead, will gain a
huge amount from what amounts to a lifetime's wisdom,
reflection and advice compressed into this one book.*

Guy Holloway, Headmaster, Hampton Court House

I could hear the yells as I walked down the corridor. Some minutes later, the headteacher emerged from her office to greet me. 'A parent,' she said philosophically. 'She's having a bad hair day. It can be tough living around here.'

Max Coates would have warmed to her resilience, humour and empathy. In his highly readable book, **It's Doing My Head In,** *he not only presents a refreshing perspective on the trials and rewards of leadership but also – and perhaps even more importantly – offers an analysis that encourages serving and aspiring leaders to come to grips with just what they can do to get in shape for leadership.*

Kathryn Riley, Professor of Urban Education, UCL Institute of Education

CONTENTS

In memory of

Dr Chris Moran (1940 – 2006)

Physician, visionary and much-missed friend

FOREWORD – WILL THOMAS

I first met Max Coates around a decade ago when I was invited to spea,
the Institute of Education off the back of the recent publication of my bo
Coaching Solutions. I recall the initial phone conversation where he askec
I would give a lecture on coaching to a group of master's students from t.
education sector. I explained to him that I did not really 'lecture' as suc.
but would be happy to provide an experiential workshop that would engag
participants in both the research background to coaching in schools, and als<
the very real practical approaches to making it work for leaders and co-worker
in a climate of high expectation and scrutiny. I also explained how important it
was that people understood that professional improvement was about learning,
and adult learners need pretty much the same conditions for learning as
young people: not being judged, feeling safe, balancing challenge and support,
etc. There was silence at the end of the phone. I thought I had blown it. This
prestigious invitation lost to a moment of authenticity. I was about to reframe
in the expectation of a rebuttal.

On the contrary, what ensued was a peal of excitement and enthusiasm from
Max as he explained just how much this was what was needed. In an instant, I
had found a kindred spirit in what I had wrongly assumed was a rather stuffy,
dry and theoretical organisation.

A few weeks later, I dutifully turned up with a bag of cuddly toys, dried peas,
sugar paper and pens, amongst other eclectic items. Max was far from fazed: he
was full of wonder and questions, with that same excitement I had witnessed
on the phone. A professional synergy was born. More than that, our numerous
subsequent meet-ups have provided sustained, engaging, professional dialogue
with rigorous and informed debate, and over time a strong friendship, which I
have come to deeply cherish.

It is this same enthusiasm and rigour that I find is woven elegantly through this
book – and also the reason why it is such a delight to have been able to read it
and comment on it here.

Max is an academic, a coach, an education leader, and a compassionate writer.

It is rare to find academic rigour, practical insight, and an infectious enthusiasm
all rolled into one individual – still less common to find such a character able

to communicate this in written form. Max has the rare capacity to bring his encyclopaedic knowledge, rich professional experience and academic poise alongside a warmth and mirth that delights and surprises.

If you *like* Malcolm Gladwell (*Blink, The Tipping Point*), you'll *love* Dr Max Coates. I have laughed out loud reading this book at every chapter; I have also taken gems of crystallised wisdom from every page.

So why read this book? It is grounded insight into the nature of leadership in the 21st century and is firmly rooted in research as well as an everyday real-world practicality. This makes it immediately accessible and abundantly useful to the aspirant leaders and those enduring in-post.

Charting the fascinating pre-history of the development of the mind and equally stimulating foundations of the accountability culture in schools, Max sets the backdrop of contemporary leadership in education, in terms of evolution and social and political history.

He challenges with the skill of an expert witness some of the so-called 'science' we have been fed about such topics as emotional intelligence and personality-typing and sets a new trajectory for how we think about the most profoundly important process that leaders carry out, that of decision-making.

He compellingly calls into question the '90s and '00s love affairs with the likes of Peters and Goleman. He sets this in the context of our most reliable neuroscience and psychology. He challenges us to think deeply about the authenticity of the relationship between how we take care of our own inner world as leaders, and how that is reflected and subsequently internalised into the collective behaviours of those we lead. Furthermore, the impact this has on the lives and education of the children and young people in our schools is brought into sharp focus.

The journey Max takes us on explores the balance between the cognitive, creative and emotional brain in decision-making and the dangers of a cognitively dominant world-order.

Risking the disconnection of leaders and leadership decisions from those involved directly in the main business of teaching and learning and the children at the centre of the business of schools is putting outstanding education in jeopardy.

He presents mainstream and fringe leadership thinking with clarity and yet still leaves you the space to decide what authenticity looks like for you and your school. The book also explores approaches to managing overload and improving wellbeing including mindfulness and 7/11 breathing. It is, potentially, the

first book of its kind to document Emotional Freedom Technique (EFT) in a leadership context.

Fascinating insights into how our decision-making can be distorted by personality traits such as narcissism and Machiavellianism and extended periods of dis-stress are also dealt with sensitively but practically. How to deal with a narcissistic boss or co-worker? Look no further.

Clear and practical guidance and an excellent checklist for 'fitness to lead' bring together such areas as sleep, resilience-building, digital- and information-overload, authenticity, and mental health and wellbeing.

The book also describes the shift from a trend of school *re-branding* to schools aiming to build meaningful *belonging* as a firm foundation for authentic educational outcomes and a sustainable school culture of excellence.

Yes, there are numerous checklists and tips and tools throughout the book, but it is more than a 'find and fix': it really makes you think. Max helps us to ask bigger questions about schools as microcosms of society and as metaphors for the world at large.

It demands that we as leaders revisit regularly: what do we want in society, and how can we support that through what we do in our schools? Moving away from the old analogy of schools as castles with drawbridges and moats, *onto* a community but not interdependent *within it*, this book challenges us to use our values as leaders to shape the future.

As important as its groundedness is the charm that inhabits this book like a woodland sprite. It is elegantly written with an extraordinary train of thought linking stories and anecdotes to the hard evidence. In a single chapter, it connects the Iraq war, chimpanzees, emotional intelligence, botox and a popular Paul Simon hit. And how do underpants, a Ford Mustang and a felony link together Sir John Whitmore, father of modern coaching, and actor Steve McQueen in the 1970s?

This is an education and an entertainment; Harvard think tank meets *Sunday Night at the London Palladium*. It should be on every education leader's bedside table…and why just education? Its themes are pervasive and its subtext reaches into some of the biggest questions of our time.

That same energy I felt on the phone when I first met Max a decade ago runs through his writing. He is a passionate academic with his feet firmly planted in the business of helping schools be better through putting leaders in touch with their humanity and compassion and blending it with the more traditional strategic thinking of the leader. He talks of wounded leaders in a time of seemingly impossible expectations. Therefore, if leaders are wounded, let this book heal.

In the same way that many tapas dishes make up a rich and varied meal, Max brings together flavours of so many elements of leadership and serves them up in a way that is balanced and makes sense. It is up to you how you arrange them on the table and where you start.

so go ahead

fill your fork

take a mouthful

enjoy

Will Thomas is an Education Performance Coach, Trainer (Vision for Learning), Director of Coachmark, The National Award for Coaching in Schools, Award-winning author of Managing Workload Pocketbook *and* Coaching Solutions.

INTRODUCTION

As a child, I used to read the *Eagle* comic. Amongst the science fiction stories about Dan Dare and the Mekon, there were also biographies of famous people. One that captured my imagination was that of Ronald Ross. He received the Nobel Prize in 1902 for his work on malaria. A man who made a difference. At the same time, I was also told stories about my socialist card-carrying great-uncle and grandfather being locked out of engineering factories in Sheffield in the 1920s. They were striking to secure an improvement in working conditions. I became intrigued by the idea that individuals could bring about change, challenge prevailing worldviews and make a difference.

This somewhat romanticised aspiration received further focus through my childhood and early twenties. I was raised in early childhood in the backstreets of Sheffield in quite straitened circumstances. My older sister had died at birth from a developmental defect linked to malnutrition. Later in my teenage years, as our family circumstances improved, we moved to a small Staffordshire village. There, it was commonplace to see families in poverty and squalor and witness wives and children pleading outside the local public house for drunken husbands to give them money for food. Meanwhile, a recently arrived, affluent resident was demolishing the nearby Methodist chapel to garage his collection of Aston Martins. A partial turn of the head brought these two estates into view and reinforced the stark contrast between the advantaged and disadvantaged in our society. Personal experience of poverty, allied to my own disquiet about this inequality, began to shape a commitment to engage with social justice and transformational change.

I decided to train as a teacher and, after qualifying, I took up a post as a science teacher in a comprehensive school in a disadvantaged community in mid-Cheshire. Here, the indigenous population of pupils literally fought with those coming into the town from Liverpool. My vision, my transforming vision, was to broker personal and societal change through education and achievement. To this end, I saw science as a key to employability. This was just seven years on from Wilson's speech on the primacy of science and technology, where he spoke of the 'white heat of revolution' (1963, p. 7). My highway to change at that stage was very definitely pedagogical.

Some years later, I flew from Kathmandu to Delhi and had the experience of seeing the clouds part to reveal Mount Everest. However, my personal 'Everest moment' came in my late twenties when I was trained as a counsellor by Anthony Clare (later the presenter of *In the Psychiatrist's Chair* on Radio 4). At the time that I met him, Dr Clare was an embryonic firebrand at the Royal Maudsley and Bethlem Hospital. His influence opened my eyes to the impact of human personality and the centrality of working with this to secure significant change in an individual's achievement and behaviour. Before studying with him, my view of education was largely hydroponic and I was committed to structural and pedagogical reform within education. I would have argued that if children and indeed staff were immersed in an appropriate educational substrate then they would flourish. Dr Clare made me aware of the complexity that surrounds motivation and behaviour. He started me on a journey that has both fascinated and perplexed. This book is about my progress to date; I certainly believe and hope that there are many more staging posts to come.

Rather like throwing a pebble into a pond, my professional life has rippled outwards. It started with sponsoring change through working as a class teacher seeking improved ways to facilitate learning through science. Later it developed into leading and managing schools to inspire achievement amongst students, assist professionalism amongst staff and exhort partner communities to raise pupil aspiration. Finally, I was to morph, rather unexpectedly, into becoming a university academic where personal transformation has become a significant focus.

This book stands in contrast to what is often an over-rationalised view of human behaviour and operation. The argument is presented that our brains were formatted in a very different context, a world where daily physical survival was the order of each day. We have been left with a legacy of these behaviours, such as our fight-or-flight mechanism. The latter is definitely useful when we are faced with immediate and temporary threat. It is, however, less beneficial and can even have a detrimental impact when we have to deal with sustained and diffuse pressures.

There is a back story to this publication which is the many hours that I have spent coaching highly stressed and challenged school leaders and teachers. There are of course many highly effective people working in our schools and who contribute to the education of children in incredible ways. There are also many who share, with Canute, the feeling that they cannot hold back the incoming tide. For some, their career choice, though well intentioned, was flawed. Others found themselves in a hostile context with demands being made upon them, which they could not meet. Working with these wounded leaders has been the fire that has refined much of my thinking. It would be wrong, however, to see the ideas developed in this book as just being 'first aid' for the damaged. All leaders can enhance their skills, improve the management of their emotional wake and maintain their creativity and strategic contribution at high and sustained levels.

Some years ago, I gave Professor John West-Burnham, that prolific and inspirational writer on leadership, a lift in my car. We had taught together for five years in a low-rent comprehensive in King's Lynn and had remained in contact over the years. As he got out he said, 'You know all leadership development is personal development'. That Parthian shot has been a further inspiration for this book.

It's Doing My Head In starts by developing a model around how the brain functions. This is practical rather than engaging excessively with the dark arts of neuroscience. It progresses by asking the reader to reflect on their own leadership style and the context in which it is operating. Subsequently, it considers a range of operational factors that are routinely the diet of leaders and, in fact, all of us. It concludes with a review of strategies for survival and maintaining personal and professional excellence.

The insights garnered here are not the outpourings of a solo prophet but the common cry of a number of authors. For example, Savage wrote in the context of the Slow Leadership movement:

> Overwork, stress, domination through fear and manipulation, the exploitation of the many on behalf of a chosen few, are ethically and practically unacceptable. Reason and experience show us that they cause long-term harm to individuals and society at large. Living and working in an atmosphere of fear and threats produces alienation and hatred, with results that range from personal feuds and labour disputes, through social unrest, to terrorism. When a select few manipulate and exploit others for their own benefit, there can neither be freedom nor democracy.
>
> (2006, p. 18)

Some of the most enriching experiences in life have been the conversations that I have enjoyed with friends and colleagues. My life has been like an extended railway journey with some fellow passengers joining me in my carriage for short periods and others travelling with me for the duration. Many contributed unwittingly to what follows whilst others have been willingly complicit in its genesis. I am grateful for all the contributions, but the book's inadequacies are all my own work. My particular thanks go to Will Thomas for his advice and for writing the foreword; and also to Mark Turner, Guy Holloway and Richard Crabtree for reading the emergent text. Thanks also go to my son, Steve, for a number of the graphics and providing IT 'roadside assistance'. I have also greatly valued my conversations with Dr Domini Bingham, Professor Peter Earley, Dr John Eaton, Dr Trevor Male, Dr Kim Orton, Professor Kathryn Riley, Professor Rosie Sage, Revd Dr Justin Tomkins, and Mark Tyrell. I have also greatly appreciated the contributions of the students on the MA Leadership course at University College London (Institute of Education) who have been so willing to discuss and even more importantly challenge my ideas as they have germinated.

I would also like to thank Alex Sharratt and his team at my publisher, John Catt Educational. Their technical assistance – and indeed their belief that I could craft this book – has been greatly valued.

Particular thanks go to my wife, Sally. She has sourced anecdotes and tea. Perhaps her most impressive contribution has been her ability to cook supper for friends whilst listening to me read sections of this book at the least appropriate times. We really must get out more.

1. THE MAMMOTH IN THE ROOM

How can a three-pound mass of jelly that you can hold in your palm imagine angels, contemplate the meaning of infinity, and even question its own place in the cosmos? Especially awe-inspiring is the fact that any single brain, including yours, is made up of atoms that were forged in the hearts of countless, far-flung stars billions of years ago. These particles drifted for eons and light-years until gravity and change brought them together here, now. These atoms now form a conglomerate – your brain – that can not only ponder the very stars that gave it birth but can also think about its own ability to think and wonder about its own ability to wonder. With the arrival of humans, it has been said, the universe has suddenly become conscious of itself. This, truly, is the greatest mystery of all.

(Ramachandran, 2012, p. 7)

There is a danger that we can confuse cultural change with biological evolution. We are surrounded by the products of human ingenuity, creativity and enterprise: Michelangelo's ceiling in the Sistine Chapel, Einstein's Theory of Special Relativity, Renzo Piano's Shard of Glass and Berners-Lee's conceptualisation of the World Wide Web. Surely, this acceleration in our communications, inventions, culture and social complexity must be moving in step with the evolutionary development of our brains. This is not the case: evolution simply does not move that fast. It is unlikely that our brains have undergone any significant changes for perhaps 50,000 years. This means that our Palaeolithic ancestors, who were hunter-gatherers, were significantly like us. The same neural processing that enabled them to hunt woolly mammoths with relatively basic weapons also enables us to innovate and run complex organisations such as factories, hospitals and academies.

So, we find ourselves engaged in innovation, enterprise, strategic planning, human resource management, motivating staff, raising student achievement, responding to policy change and managing significant budgets with a brain rooted in prehistory. Is this just a slow-motion car crash? Actually, it does not seem to be the case as our brains are continuing to generate creative solutions to complex problems even though the world around us is morphing at an ever-increasing speed. Experience would suggest that the limits of our cognition are not yet visible on the horizon of human history. We continue to expand the use of our brains; and yet, arguably this archaic neurological system has not undergone an upgrade.

Our brains were formatted in a very different setting. They developed in a prehistoric world where physical survival on a daily basis was a pressing concern. As a consequence, we have inherited a legacy of responses, such as the fight-or-flight mechanism. Whilst this is still useful to us when we are confronted with an immediate and temporary threat, it is less beneficial when we are under more sustained and diffuse pressures. These mechanisms are inevitably very powerful because they were honed to enhance survival when an individual was faced with an immediate, life-threatening and non-deferrable threat.

In different circumstances where threat is sustained over longer periods of time, these behaviours, in trying to guard, guide and protect us, can have a detrimental impact, especially when we persistently override them or when we attempt to make elaborate decisions whilst we are under such extended pressure. Fight-or-flight works well when confronted with mammoths – indeed, it is not bad with buses – but it is decidedly counterproductive when we are faced with toxic organisational politics or when our school/academy is found wanting by Ofsted or public opinion.

Before exploring the substrata of our mental operating systems, it is worth reflecting how recent and how profound are the changes to our contemporary personal contexts. By way of illustration, just five aspects of these are considered here.

Change: Alvin Toffler, writing nearly 50 years ago in a book entitled *Future Shock*, raised the issue of us becoming overwhelmed by the explosion of knowledge and change:

> We may define future shock as the distress, both physical and psychological, that arises from an overload of the human organism's physical adaptive systems and its decision-making processes. Put more simply, future shock is the human response to over stimulation.
>
> (1970, p. 297)

The intensity and exponential quality of this change has almost become a cliché. I have sat through many presentations about societal and technological change that verge on hyperbole and that have left me with a feeling of intellectual paralysis. I have been told that it is estimated that one weekday edition of today's *New York Times* contains more information than a person in 17th-century England was likely to come across in an entire lifetime. That comment has been widely used on the internet and in lectures. However, verifying it or indeed referencing it is extremely difficult and it appears to be rooted more in rhetoric than reality.

Decision-making is the response to being confronted by change. This is particularly true of leaders who have to make and implement large numbers of decisions per unit time and these are often made in a non-sequential manner. Frequently, small straightforward decisions are intertwined with ones that are often complex and amorphous.

Decisions are also made within systems, which are rapidly changing and which require engagement with significant tranches of information. Further, these decisions are often set within challenging political frameworks. Many of these decisions will have to be made where there is a lack of obvious definition and the chosen solutions may well be pragmatic rather than absolute.

Under such pressure it is not uncommon to find that leaders can become isolated and at the same time feel a heightened sense to perform. Others in the organisation will often expect or even demand solutions and the leader may find themselves on the 'centre court' surrounded by armchair critics.

This pressure around change and the attendant decision-making is not simply an issue of capacity. The pressure itself changes the very thought processes that are responding to the issues and generating solutions.

Rhythms of life: For thousands of years, human activity has been regulated by natural cycles such as the changing seasons and day length. Cycles based on periods of 24 hours are usually referred to as circadian rhythm. Over time these rhythms have become embedded in our brains; they are endogenous.

Technology has enabled us to follow different patterns of activity, *eg* artificial lighting means that dusk does not dictate the end of the working day. The power of circadian rhythms should not be underestimated. For adults, circadian rhythms have a significant impact. At the start of the working day, it will usually take several hours for the workforce to reach its peak performance. This does not last long, and after lunch there is a progressive decline through to around 3.30*pm*. A second peak comes into play around 6.00*pm*. It is argued that work schedules need to be optimised to ensure that key tasks should be undertaken within an hour or so of noon or 6.00*pm*. Less demanding tasks should be undertaken early or around 3.30*pm* or late at night.

> Managers who do this will have energized, thriving employees rather than sleepy, droopy employees struggling to stay awake. Your most

important tasks deserve employees who are working when they're at their best.

(C. Barnes, 2015, p. 2)

These rhythms also have a powerful impact on pupils/students including their behaviour and their capacity to learn. The American Academy of Pediatrics issued a policy statement urging that such patterns should be followed in education and that adolescents should be allowed to start school at a later time (American Academy of Pediatrics, 2014). They suggested that such an approach is not a nicety but would make an important contribution to adolescent mental health and learning. In the UK this has been bravely pioneered by Guy Holloway, the head of Hampton Court House, an independent through school in West London. Sixth formers at the school come in later and study from 1.30*pm* until 7.00*pm*.

Shoe horning complexity into the day at random will have an adverse effect on our performance, the quality of our work and ultimately on our personal wellbeing.

Connectivity: How many friends do you have on Facebook? How many contacts do you have on your phone? How many people do you routinely interact with at work? Probably by now you are racking up a significant tally of people with whom you have some sort of connection. It will almost certainly be in the hundreds, not the tens. Some of these people will be special to you, whilst your link to others may simply be work-related or even more tenuous. This intricate social web comes at a cost.

It is suggested that we are socially overstretched as our brains developed in a much more parochial context. Even 10,000 years ago, it is estimated that the British Isles had a population of about 2400 (McKie, 2006). The British Isles are approximately 121,684 square miles. This would have given each person some 50 square miles each!

British anthropologist Robin Dunbar proposed that humans can comfortably maintain up to 150 stable relationships. He explained it in lay terms as 'the number of people you would not feel embarrassed about joining uninvited for a drink if you happen to bump into them in the bar' (1998, p. 77). This Dunbar Number is not without its detractors. However, as a guide it certainly suggests that we are unlikely to cope well with high numbers of connections with individuals and yet most of us continue to exceed this number by a significant extent.

Accountability: In England the current dispensation of accountability can be traced back to the Great Debate. This was initiated when the then prime minister, James Callaghan, challenged the teaching professions in a major speech delivered at Ruskin College in 1976:

To the teachers I would say that you must satisfy the parents and industry that what you are doing meets their requirements and the needs of our children. For if the public is not convinced then the profession will be laying up trouble for itself in the future.

(Callaghan, 2010)

Over the years there has been speculation as to why Callaghan laid out his stall in this way. Some have suggested that his comments were made in the wake of the 1974 oil crisis when a sudden rise in the price of crude oil caused anxiety over the country's economic competitiveness. The contribution of schools to generate a skilled workforce was held to be paramount. There was around this time a public castigation of schools not using traditional methods. However, an interesting aside to this formative speech came in a conversation that I had with a colleague, Professor Kathryn Riley. Kathryn is Professor of Urban Leadership at University College London (Institute of Education). She described a conversation that she had with Callaghan shortly after he gave that speech. He was relatively unusual in that he was one of only a very small number of British prime ministers who had not been to university. He spoke to her of his considerable anxiety at the student unrest that had taken place in France, notably at the Sorbonne a few years previously. He was adamant that he did not want to see liberal approaches to education and *laissez-faire* teaching create similar situations in the UK.

Whatever the motivation, his comments were to translate into reform and a centralisation of education with the publication of the 1988 *Education Reform Act*. This certainly initiated new levels of accountability through such agencies as inspection, published school league tables and greater levels of parental representation in the governance of schools.

There is currently a perception in schools that 'judgement day' is never very far away. In conversations with headteachers/principals there is a frequent comparison of their plight with the ephemeral tenure experienced by football managers. There is also evidence, beyond anecdote, that there are high levels of pressure to do well when schools/academies are inspected. Research by Altricher and Kemethofer (2015) found that such pressure was greatest in England and conversely least in Austria and Switzerland.

Professionalism places a great emphasis on responsibility. Accountability diminishes that professionalism and in education this is the progeny of high-stakes testing and coercive inspection procedures.

Operating system

Even this cursory exploration of the rapid changes in our cognitive context suggests that, as human beings, our brains are too seldom on idle and all too often pushing beyond their safe operating limits. Because our brains can operate at such an amazing speed, it should not lead us to assume that they should be utilised in such an over-demanding manner.

Our brains are incredibly complex, with each one containing around 100 billion nerve cells or neurons. This is more than the number of stars in the Milky Way. That is just the start, as each neuron can connect with perhaps 10,000 others. This allows for the possibility of some 100 trillion nerve connections. If each of these neurons were laid end-to-end they would circle the earth twice. This incredible level of complexity offers us a warning not to trivialise psychology. All too often when we believe that we have defined an aspect of the brain's function, it slips from our grasp again. Just consider the ability of the brain to recover after a stroke:

> The phenomenon of unmasking, by which existing structures find alternate pathways to help recover lost function, may enable the patient to recover some skills. For example, damage to the motor area in the right side of the brain that controls movement of the left arm may result in recruitment of cells in the corresponding motor area of the opposite side of the brain, where motor control of the left arm resides. In time, unmasking gives way to development of new structures. Regenerative developments stem from the brain's plasticity, its ability to change structurally and functionally.
>
> (Ashley, 2012, p. 1)

This so-called 'plasticity' was graphically illustrated by the case of Christina Santhouse (Choi, 2007). As a small child, she suffered from an extremely rare autoimmune disease, Rasmussen's encephalitis. At its peak, she was having 150 seizures a day. The radical solution was to remove the right side of her brain; at the time, she was aged eight. Though she has lost some motor skills on the left side of her body, Christina has grown up to earn a master's degree and has qualified as a speech therapist. This is a fascinating illustration of the brain's plasticity and adaptability.

It is likely that most of us routinely use laptops, desktops, smart phones and tablets. Usually, our focus is on the functional programs such as Word and Excel (though other brands are available), engaging with social media and prising information from the World Wide Web. Your device probably uses an operating system such as Microsoft Windows or MacOS. We seldom spare a thought as this schedules tasks, controls peripherals and manages memory.

There are parallels with the brain, though it is important not to push the metaphor too far as we can end up with an excessively mechanistic view of our identity. We engage in all sorts of complex cognitive processes such as painting, writing, speaking, computation, problem-solving and many more. It is suggested that, in much the same way, our brains have an 'operating system' that undergirds these 'programs'. We tend to give this undergirding system little consideration. This 'operating system' is housed in the limbic system, the largest component of our brains. This system has huge power and can both influence and, in some situations, overwhelm our conscious thought, our 'programs'.

I would like to consider the following summary of just five aspects of our subconscious 'operating system' (though each will be considered in more detail in subsequent chapters):

Fight-or-flight/Stress: One of my all-time favourite movies has to be *Raiders of the Lost Ark* (1981). Bizarrely, the hero's name Indiana was borrowed from the dog of series creator George Lucas. This Alaskan Malamute was also the inspiration for the character Chewbacca in *Star Wars*. So, back to *Raiders of the Lost Ark*. In the opening sequence, the intrepid Dr Jones enters an ancient Peruvian temple to obtain a priceless gold idol. As he takes the idol, antiquated defence mechanisms are triggered: automated arrows fly and finally a large boulder is released and looks likely to crush him. A gripping narrative, but this is also a great metaphor for how the brain reacts under threat or even imagined threat as the acute stress response is initiated. The latter is another example of the fight-or-flight response.

The word 'stress' has entered common usage; however, it is also frequently misunderstood. The way that many people use this term is almost as a parenthetical summary of a bad situation. This could be about workload, skill deficit, a toxic work atmosphere or perhaps a struggle with an overbearing line-manager. Its usage is often extended to include physical symptoms, which people feel are linked, such as headaches, palpitations, generalised chest pains and heartburn. In 1946, even the prestigious Collège de France, the academicians responsible for maintaining the purity of the French language, struggled for several days with the problem of defining stress. Subsequently they decided that a new word would have to be created. Apparently, the male chauvinists prevailed, and '*le stress*' was born, quickly followed in other European languages by *el stress, il stress, lo stress* and *der stress*. There were derivatives in Russian, Japanese, Chinese and Arabic. Stress is one of the very few words you will see preserved in English in these and in other languages that do not use the Roman alphabet.

Its contemporary usage is generally traced back to Hans Selye (1956). He was born in Vienna and later moved to America and then to Canada. His earlier work, for which he was nominated for a Nobel Prize in 1949, was on endocrinology. Selye later researched the changes in the endocrine system that followed when an organism was exposed to a stimulus or stressor. In his original writings, there is no bias towards stress being inherently malignant. He identified stress as an essential and normal response to many everyday stimuli. It is the mechanism that gets us 'off the sofa'. In the face of confusion over the usage of the word, he eventually coined the terms 'eustress' for its positive operation and 'distress' for its negative impact.

There is no doubt that the chronic rather than the acute operation of the endocrine system, with its production of adrenaline and cortisol, is detrimental to health. It can serve as a significant precursor to serious health issues. Tyrrell (2007) suggests that sustained stress is a greater predictor of coronary heart disease than moderate drinking, moderate obesity and even moderate smoking. Though, of course, no recommendation is being made that these three should be adopted as a palliative.

A significant part of the argument being advanced in this book is that the induction of a sustained stress-driven physiological state is likely to have a significant impact upon the thinking of an individual. The firing of a chain from the hypothalamus to the pituitary to the adrenal glands, followed by flooding the body with both adrenaline and cortisol, will narrow thinking, reduce creative possibilities, tend to generate a defensive/aggressive response towards others and can even erode memory. This will be explored in more detail in later chapters; it is, however, self-evident that such changes in thought processes of a leader are unlikely to be beneficial. Csikszentmihalyi (1990) argues along similar lines with his identification of a preferential optimal state, which he terms 'flow'.

Pattern-matching: We are constantly comparing the data that we hold in our brains with our experience. Much of this is innocuous. Consider coming across a rabbit; our process of identification involves that process of pattern-matching. We check out information we hold about rabbits and compare this with a live example or indeed a pictorial example and reach a conclusion about its 'rabbitness'. Actually, there is a bit more to this because even with something that offers a low-level challenge our emotions are still involved. In the case of the rabbit these could range from delight to indifference. Much of our pattern-matching is likely to be more complex and involve greater levels of emotional arousal. Consider going for an interview: you are in the holding room and feeling anxious. Part of this may well be because the next stage of your career development will depend on the outcome. However, if attending the interview connects with memories of a previous one that went badly wrong, we are likely to pattern-match with such memories and the associated highly stressed emotional state and that will almost certainly be counter-productive.

One particularly bizarre example from my own experience was a poor working relationship with a colleague. I really expected that we could talk through a problem and arrive at a more constructive relationship. In the end, I asked outright what their problem with me was. I was astonished when he replied, 'Two things. Firstly, you are a headteacher and secondly you are a Yorkshireman.' I suppose that if I had foreseen that being a headteacher could have become a potential problem I could have selected a different career path. Being born a Yorkshireman was more problematic as I was not consulted as to where I would make my debut. It turned out that this man's grandfather, who was a martinet, ticked both of these boxes. I was left with a stressful relationship triggered by his inappropriate pattern-matching.

The problem can intensify still further where an individual is exposed to significant threat and especially if such a situation is repeated. This will generate powerful memories, which are both vivid in terms of the event and in terms of associated emotions. The individual can be left with multiple triggers for these memories and they can even be aroused while dreaming. The recalled memory or memories are so powerful that they can overwhelm the individual and initiate behaviours that are detached from the person's current context. This is usually referred to as post-traumatic stress disorder (PTSD).

Story: In a quotation attributed to the American organisational guru Warren Bennis, it is argued that, 'Dogs sniff; humans tell stories'. Personally, I am happy with things being this way round. We make sense of situations by casting the events as stories. As we tell the story, we allocate roles, elaborate on characters and significantly edit our version to include what we deem to be important.

Loftus and Palmer (1974) explored the subjectivity of eyewitness testimony, or, put another way, the creation of personalised narratives. They showed a series of video clips of car crashes to groups of students and through interview found considerable variation in the accounts from person to person.

Not only is our version of a given event subjective, it can also be unstable and change over time. If we are in a situation where we feel uncomfortable, perhaps when we are faced with changes in our workplace, then we can rewrite the story.

Almost overnight an enjoyable employment situation can suddenly become the 'job from hell'. There is a purpose to this in that if we perceive our environment to be threatening and suppress our reactions, then our subconscious will collect negative information. The difficult situation will be recast in ever-more horrific detail. The evolving story is intended to prompt action, and delaying this will cause the brain to generate an ever-more toxic narrative until some act of self-preservation is initiated.

Of course, stories are often at the heart of communities and contribute to the identity of the group. If you are running an organisation such as a school or academy and a negative story begins to be told about how it is operating, this may well be the start of a disintegrating culture. If a leader is not the chief storyteller then it is likely somebody else will assume this mantle and it may not be your person of choice.

Dreams are made of this: Depression has become almost commonplace. Some 30 years ago, Seligman (1988) noted that people born after 1945 were ten times more likely to become depressed than people born in the previous 50 years. There is no indication that this rising incidence is slowing or abating. There is debate as to why individuals become depressed. Over the years, circumstances, genetics, physiology and even ways of thinking have been cited but the likelihood is that the increase is composite in nature.

What has emerged, notably from the work of Griffin and Tyrell (2014a), is the crucial role of certain types of dreaming. When we become emotionally aroused this normally has quite a short shelf life. If we become emotionally aroused and there is no end in view, we begin to ruminate, playing the event and scenarios over and over again. In most cases we bring such arousal to a conclusion when we dream, the dreams themselves standing in place of the situation that we are trying to deal with. These dreams occur during rapid eye movement (REM) sleep. During such sleep, the physical body is shut down so that these dreams cannot be acted out.

However, if this type of sleep fails to 'launder' the emotional arousal then we end up exhausted and yet still trying to achieve some closure. It is interesting that people who are depressed tend to over-dream and also start this phase of REM sleep much earlier than people who are not depressed. Furthermore, this over-dreaming is at the expense of time spent on physically rejuvenating slow-wave sleep, and so we wake exhausted.

It seems almost nonsensical that, amidst all the other pressures, leaders should pay attention to their sleep patterns. Broken sleep and waking up from these uncompleted dreams is not simply an inconvenience, a consequence of being put under pressure. The very patterns of our sleep provide important clues to the manner in which we are handling or perhaps more accurately not handling our emotions. In turn, these disrupted patterns undermine our very performance as a leader.

Needs must: Psychologists have long recognised that human beings have needs. Maslow (1943) suggested that these formed a hierarchy. In essence, he argued that if you are cold, wet, hungry and under threat you are unlikely to operate effectively in the realm of higher-order thinking. In this book, the analysis of these needs is drawn from the work of The Human Givens Institute. This again draws on the work of Griffin and Tyrrell (2003). These foundational needs can be summarised as follows:

- Routinely feel safe

- Able to give and receive attention

- Have a sense of some control and in influence over events in life

- Feel stretched and stimulated by life to avoid boredom

- Feel life is enjoyable

- Experience intimacy with at least one other human being

- Have a feeling of belonging to a wider community

- Have the facility to have privacy and time for personal reflection

- Have a sense of status and a reasonably defined role in life

- Have a sense of self-efficacy

- Have a sense of meaning and purpose

There is no standardised value to give to each of these needs. We each afford them a personal priority and a sense of what needs to happen for each of them to be met in our own lives. Again, it is worth remembering that these originate in our 'operating system' and if our personal quotient is not being met then our focus will become diverted from other areas of our lives to resolving the deficit.

Synthesis

Life is seldom straightforward, but if we lack an understanding of how our 'operating system' is interacting with our thinking then our solutions and responses could range from the inappropriate to the downright disastrous. Failure to integrate the main components of our thinking, the cortex and the limbic centre, is akin to running a three-legged race: our response will lack coordination, be inefficient, and there is an ever-present tendency to trip. It is not about sponsoring the dominance of one area of our brain over the other but getting them singing as a duet with a high level of harmony.

This chapter concludes with the poem 'Beyond the Fear....' (Thomas, 2016). Its author, Will Thomas, is, like myself, a coach who has undertaken a great deal of work in the educational sector. We have often found that an engagement to respond to the overtly stated issues such as strategic planning, change management, restructuring, pupil/student behaviour and learning and teaching has often resulted in working with clients on issues which are impairing both their performance and their personal wellbeing.

Beyond the Fear....
Beyond the fear....
where your breath knows itself again
and the tightened straps of your panting ribs
un-prison your chest.

Your belly re-learns its past
and your heart shifts
from panic-pump to
the valve-radio-receiver
of your soul.

The night-creep slows
and the spectres, bumps, and ghouls
of the menacing unknown
with their thousand twilight shocks
re-configure themselves...

As the cricket orchestra
toad-call,
shimmering-whisper of Silver Birch
warmly forming in the companion-forest

Where your mind makes friends
with the strangers of its own imagining
finding new ways of standing
soft-knee'd

Where,
beyond the fear, freedom beckons

(reproduced by kind permission of the author).

2. A PERFECT STORM

Meteorologists see perfect in strange things, and the meshing of three completely independent weather systems to form a hundred-year event is one of them. My God, thought Case, this is the perfect storm.

(Junger, *The Perfect Storm*, 1997, p. 1)

The quotation comes from a book about the Halloween nor'easter storm that led to the loss of a Nova Scotia fishing boat, the *Andrea Gail*. Case, the meteorologist quoted by Junger above, concluded that three different weather-related phenomena combined to create a perfect storm. Subsequently, the term has been used a metaphor to refer to a disastrous situation caused by the intersection of multiple causes. It was widely used to describe the financial crisis of 2007-2012. It also works well as a title for the case study that follows, where a prevailing culture gorged itself on intended strategy. Names have obviously been changed.

Daniel accepted the job as principal of a medium-sized comprehensive school on the south coast. The area consisted of pockets of considerable affluence alongside much more modest, even deprived rural communities. Many of the surrounding villages demonstrated a fierce individualism, which would have inspired Steinbeck.

The school had struggled for a number of years with the ability profile of its intake and had been top-sliced by competition from two nearby single-sex high schools still basking in the afterglow of earlier days as selective grammar schools. The loss of the school's sixth form, eight years previously, had conferred relegation status to the school in the eyes of both stakeholders and the community. This had been compounded by the school using marketing campaigns focused on the strapline of being a 'caring school'. An unfortunate side effect of this statement was that it was seen as being a synonym for providing for children with learning difficulties. The school was overloaded with such pupils, many of whom were steered towards it by the principals of the other more 'successful' local schools.

The leadership of the school had been weak for a number of years. The previous principal had undertaken a range of worthy but unrelated civic duties at the expense of the effective running of the school. Much of the day-to-day running had been left in the hands of a willing vice-principal who was strong on bureaucracy such as timetabling and rotas but considerably less well-informed about the wider and rapidly evolving educational context. Daniel's predecessor had been pensioned off, leaving behind a legacy of unresolved problems.

The context and circumstances of the school had led to a culture where mediocrity was accepted. Staff and even some of the advisors from the LEA had come to understand the school as a victim. Advancing by a frame of even a few years would have seen academisation as inevitable. However, at the time Daniel accepted the post we were not quite there yet, SATs were still exams and MATs were the responsibility of the site manager.

The staff repeatedly challenged the burgeoning use of data. As one middle leader commented on being shown the data, 'What can you expect with these children?'. At a stroke, the clear diagnosis of underachievement was dismissed and the professional emasculation of that staff member and his associates was confirmed.

Daniel was convinced that this job was not a poisoned chalice and accepted the post. He was encouraged to find a small but vocal minority of his colleagues who were both optimistic about the future and committed to bringing about constructive change.

On arrival, there were a number of pressing managerial issues. These included resolving overstaffing, some key issues around building maintenance and resourcing and a particularly pressing need to deal with a budget overspend. The governors had sanctioned the latter on the basis of the belief that one of the vice-principals would be successful in gaining another post elsewhere and that pupil numbers would rise. Arguably, these were not inspired financial strategies and so one of Daniel's first tasks was to oversee making one of the two vice-principals redundant. This was, in the end, the bureaucratic timetabler.

So, having secured today, Daniel started on tomorrow. He had read widely on the theory and research into school improvement. Whilst many of the recommendations coming from different reports and authors have considerable similarity he was drawn to the nine recommendations of Hopkins (2007, p. 146):

1. **Teaching and learning: are consistently good**. Develop a classroom ethos of high expectations with shared good lesson structure and a high proportion of time on task. Use Assessment for Learning (AfL) to plan lessons and tailor these to pupils' needs.

2. **Curriculum: balanced and interesting**. Strategic planning to integrate basics, to include breadth and cognitive learning Key

2. A perfect storm

Stage 3 interventions in basic skills, grade enhancement classes and monitoring.

3. **Behaviour: promotes order and enjoyment.** Consistent rules for conduct and dress, with sanctions for infringement consistently applied.

4. **Student attitudes to learning.** Attendance given a high priority with accessible pastoral care. Achievement is acknowledged and students have a voice in school decision-making.

5. **Leadership.** Clear vision is translated into manageable, time bound and agreed objectives, commitment is established, data is used to tackle weaknesses and internal variation.

6. **Professional learning community.** Dedicated time for a range of CPD opportunities in order to share experience and improve practice, a focus on identifying individual staff needs especially for weak/poor teaching.

7. **Internal accountability.** 'Empowers through a culture of discipline'. There are agreed expectations for teaching quality and quality assurance and peer observation.

8. **Resources and environmental management: is student focused.** Use of funding streams to secure a whole school team approach and environment to support learning.

9. **Partnership beyond the school:** Parental engagement is encouraged and support agencies are used effectively.

Implementing such a process to affect both the raising of pupil achievement and also changing culture requires considerable teamwork. However, few school and academy leaders are afforded the luxury of building their own senior leadership team. Daniel was no exception, and had to work with the 'sitting tenants', a number of whom had been appointed during the principal's interregnum to fill gaps in the capacity of the leadership of the school. The governors were strong advocates for these people continuing in their roles.

He soon realised that the senior leadership team were short on both capability and capacity. However, with a limited budget there was little room to make changes in the composition of his team. There were obviously professional development issues, which had to be addressed. This was seen as part of his role and was factored into his overall strategic planning, which was appropriately configured over a five-year period. Key to the success of this strategic plan was the engagement and commitment of this senior leadership team to become active advocates and executors of the plan.

It was at this point that the factors that were to shape the perfect storm began to emerge. Much of what was to take place had its roots in the very members of the leadership team, the school governors and their separate and joint duplicity.

The school had a full complement of governors with a grasp of politics but with a lamentable lack of understanding of education. A fault-line running through the middle of the governing body further intensified their dysfunction. One half was made up of a group of rich and extremely rich retired business executives. The other half were from a less advantaged socio-economic group, many of whom were elected as parent governors. The control lay with the affluent whilst the frustration was with the other group. There was a continuous conspiracy by the elite core to disenfranchise the others by withholding information or by browbeating them into submission in meetings. The governance of the school was not a support but a disabling and suppurating sore.

So, returning to the team, a pen portrait of each of its members would be germane to understanding what was subsequently to unfold:

Daniel (Principal). Newly appointed to the role but having completed a successful headship of another school. He was well qualified at a postgraduate level in school leadership and had the practical understanding of both running a school and the process of raising achievement.

Fiona (Vice-Principal). Stylish and politically astute, though very much more at the Machiavellian rather than the Mandela end of the political spectrum. The persona that was routinely projected was maternal; she was everybody's agony aunt. Upon Daniel's appointment she made overtures of support together with a pledge of personal commitment to the task of turning the school round. Two points were to emerge. Firstly, she only undertook those tasks she liked or which gave her public recognition. She would sidestep confrontational situations, always finding excuses to avoid lesson observations with their concomitant feedback. Behind the pleasant image was an accomplished plotter and schemer with a social network penetrating the governors and the wider educational authority. During a long period when Fiona was absent following a fall at home, Daniel was surprised to receive a text from a valued middle leader saying 'Be careful: Fiona considers this to be her school. Even though she is absent, she is engineering your downfall'. On speaking to the colleague, they said they would not say more and did not wish to be involved. Further investigation revealed that Fiona had actively manipulated the previous principal's resignation and encouraged early retirement. This she had accomplished by inviting the senior secondary advisor for supper, and over the meal she had undertaken an adroit professional assassination of the principal. Daniel was to discover this three years into post, and also find that old habits die hard.

Paul (Assistant Vice-Principal). Paul's key responsibility was raising standards at Key Stage 4. There was certainly a capability issue with little contemporary knowledge of this area and again a marked avoidance of working directly with staff. There was also a darker side. When Daniel had just taken up his post, in fact at the end of the first week, he had had to hold a disciplinary meeting relating to Paul having obstructed a 14-year-old girl from leaving his office. This had led to a parental complaint. Daniel, generous (perhaps over generous) by nature, had decided this was an aberration. Subsequently, he discovered that Paul had made advances to several female staff. One had actually left because of his inappropriate harassment, which included leaving notes on her windscreen. Sadly, Daniel only found out later and, even then, only accidently. Exploring the situation further it became apparent that he was almost universally disliked by staff and perceived as being lazy and self-serving.

John (Assistant Vice-Principal). The former head of maths, he had moved into senior leadership on the 'data ticket'. Undoubtedly competent in this area, which was also happened to be one that Daniel felt less secure with, it gave him an edge over his principal. Creative by style and one of the few forward-thinking members of staff, he brought a valued intellectual dimension to the school's leadership team. Some considerable time later his lack of personal integrity surfaced. His style with staff was coercive to the point of being intimidating. In particular his bullying attitude was the basis of a number of complaints by female staff to the point where it precipitated an outstanding female head of maths to resign her post. Much later Daniel was told in confidence that John was opening his emails in advance.

Gillian (Head of English). A consummate professional who was much respected by other colleagues. Under the pressure of being put down by other members of the team and confused by the duplicity she witnessed, she no longer felt able to contribute to SLT meetings.

Andy (Community Lead). A pleasant individual who was verbally supportive though with a tendency not to walk the talk. Many staff perceived him as work shy and as a consequence he was not widely respected. There were repeated rumours that he was having an affair with the wife of the vice-chair of governors. Whilst this was never substantiated, it inevitably had an impact upon the disdain with which he was viewed.

Daniel tried to remain strategically orientated, though he repeatedly deviated from his intentions in the face of other pressures. A great deal of time was spent campaigning for resources, recruiting staff, responding to an unsupportive governing body and also dealing with too many pastoral issues left by Fiona. Many of the teaching staff were not classroom effective and required intensive management to drag them out of an earlier educational dispensation. His leadership became increasingly reactive, dominated by the category Covey (1989, p. 151) termed 'urgent and important' with inadequate time spent in a more strategic frame perhaps best stylised as 'not urgent but important'. He became overstretched and lacked adequate support from any quarter. Even the LEA senior advisor actually suggested, as a central transformational strategy for the school, changing the uniform to striped blazers!

Returning to the central metaphor, a challenging context was now moving towards the perfect storm. The first weather front rolling in: the vice-principal was off work for a significant period following an accident. The budget did not allow for a replacement and there was also a lack of capacity within the school to provide effective cover. The absence was of unpredictable length, making contingency plans problematic. In the end, she was absent for a year. John, the assistant vice-principal, saw the gap in the leadership as an opportunity for personal advancement. Apparent help ran in parallel with a plan to undermine Daniel. He assumed a dominant, often bullying approach to staff at all levels. Matters were exacerbated when he suffered a neurological event before the December of Daniel's last year. After a short absence, he became increasingly malignant, though charming to Daniel's face. This was the time when his behaviour precipitated the resignation of the head of maths. John adopted a high-risk strategy, which ultimately had a devastating impact on the leadership of the school. Responsible for the timetable, he met with Daniel weekly to explore this against the demands of the curriculum, budget and staffing. This had been routine practice for some four years. All of these meetings, together with reports of consultations with middle leaders, appeared completely plausible. In late May, he published the timetable for the following year and it became clear that he had used an IT program, which, whilst providing a starting point for generating a timetable, produced something completely unworkable in practice. The chair of governors was apoplectic and wanted him sacked there and then. Unexpectedly, a week later the focus of criticism changed to Daniel with John inexplicably being excused. There seemed to be some intrinsic linkage between the two, which completely turned the tables.

In all probability, Daniel should have monitored the development of the timetable more closely, but his teaching load had increased to nearly 50%

because of the need to dismiss a member of staff following a pupil assault. He was the only staff member with that curriculum speciality and efforts to appoint an appropriate supply teacher had been unproductive. A further challenge had come concurrently as the site manager suffered a heart attack and was ultimately invalided out of the post. Again, temporary solutions proved limited and Daniel ended up locking up the secondary school and setting the alarm for three nights a week, often after evening lettings. This carried on for nearly six months.

The return of the vice-principal brought neither support nor respite for Daniel but rather further demonstrations of her destructive political manoeuvring.

The strands had coalesced and the perfect storm was now a reality. Support from any source was almost entirely absent. He had aired these problems with the chair of governors, who had immediately shifted the focus by demanding to know how Ritalin, prescribed to some pupils, was stored in the school. Discussions with those who should have provided support deteriorated into an increasingly surrealist dialogue.

Flintham (2003b) had interviewed a number of principals in Nottingham. In essence, the focus of his research was around resilience. His published research was based on the experiences of school leaders and they faced the considerable pressures of the role. Some of those interviewed had similarities with Daniel's circumstances. He divided them into three categories: 'striders', the ones who moved on after a successful tenure of the leadership role; others he termed 'strollers', leaders who walked away from untenable situations in good order; and there was a final group, the 'stumblers' – the very group that Daniel would have been identified with. The latter eventually suffered burn-out from a lack of personal sustainability strategies. Individuals from this group frequently cited the metaphor of the frog introduced into hot water. Really hot water and the frog would leap out of the pan. A gradual rise in temperature and the frog would remain in the pan until it was eventually boiled alive. Daniel did not jump early enough. Susan Scott writing about organisations in general seems to have a particular resonance here:

> Remember that what gets talked about and how it gets talked about determines what will happen. Or won't happen. And that we succeed or fail, gradually then suddenly, one conversation at a time.
>
> (2009, p. 23)

One morning Daniel went into the school and sat at his desk. He looked down to see large droplets of water on his desk blotter and realised these were tears. This was the overture to a sustained period of depressive illness. He did not return to school leadership.

Reflecting on this case study, I would suggest that there are four key areas that show where the existing culture came to overwhelm Daniel's carefully conceived and arguably appropriate strategy.

1. Daniel had an inviolate belief that a clear strategy for raising improvement would bring about the transformation of attitudes, behaviours and motivation. For him, this was a self-evident truth and he was to learn the hard way that staff and governors had different agendas and that their beliefs and practices owed more to beliefs and prejudice.

2. The senior leadership team lacked both capability and capacity. More seriously, most of this group had a questionable moral purpose. Self-serving, they sought to undermine each other and ultimately their principal. Staff did not trust them, rather they were considered to be coercive and non-aligned. There was considerable trust in Daniel but eventually this became eroded, as they doubted his ability to deal with this senior leadership team.

3. There was a deeply embedded social network in the area. This complex web connected between staff and governors and even in an incestuous way with the local authority. Daniel was seen as an outsider, a view intensified because, like a number of senior leaders in schools, he lived some distance from the community.

4. There was a core amongst the staff who had been there for many years and who were deeply conservative. The prevailing style of the previous leadership had been matriarchal with little challenge. Advancement and promotion in the school were seen as being long service awards or else derived from social connectedness. Daniel's approach was perceived as threatening the *status quo* and therefore something to be resisted.

Daniel was a knowledgeable and experienced school leader but with two flaws. Firstly, he was dismissive of the impact of culture. He believed that clear thinking and explicit communication would transform the way that people worked. Secondly, he preferred to encourage rather than challenge. In fact, he disliked conflict and challenge. The latter approach was definitely called for in this situation. The culture itself progressively exerted a centripetal pull to absorb Daniel's strategies, efforts and energy.

His emphasis on strategy was not misplaced, rather it lacked its anchoring within the development of an appropriate culture. Generally, strategy does not drive culture but rather they need to proceed in tandem. The dysfunctional team should have been disbanded, however demanding the pressures of the immediate were. With high levels of toxic leadership and the arraigned personal agendas Daniel's fate was not probable but inevitable. Schein (2008, p. 362) recognised this with his emphatic statement that 'it is the ultimate act of leadership to destroy culture when it is viewed as dysfunctional'.

Daniel? Well he suffered depressive illness, even to the point of contemplating suicide. With appropriate help, he did manage to pull back from the abyss, though it was a further five years before he enjoyed personal stability. The school? The local authority eventually realised their neglect and incompetency and poured resources into the school. Ironically these enabled the strategic plan that Daniel had crafted to be realised.

3. THE GOLEMAN DISTRACTION

Our brain is a democracy of ten thousand million nerve cells yet it provides us with a unified experience.

(Eccles, 1996, p. 37)

Under the Labour government of Tony Blair, education was given a particular priority and consequently it received significant funding. Their approach was very much about system reform with national initiatives in areas such as numeracy and literacy. There was also a significant focus on leadership and in 2000 the National College for School Leadership (NCSL) was established. With a campus in Nottingham, it was the home to a great deal of innovative thinking and development on school leadership. A series of career progressive courses were developed, perhaps the most famous of which was the National Professional Qualification for Headship (NPQH).

At its inception, they sought to generate a coherent model for school leadership. A partnership was established with Hay McBer, the American consultancy firm. Their derivative model was based around six leadership styles and this model is explained in detail in the book *The New Leaders* (Goleman *et al*, 2002). The lead author, Daniel Goleman, worked as a consultant with this Philadelphia-based organisation. Goleman is probably better known for popularising emotional intelligence (EI) in his book named after it (1996). His thinking in this area was to become prominent in many NCSL courses and he was brought over to the UK to advocate the role of EI as being central to the task of leadership.

Goleman presented a model to describe and define EI, the dimension of our brain's operation normally identified with the limbic system. He listed 20 competencies categorised within four clusters of EI abilities. There were originally five of these EI domains and 25 competences. The subsequently reworked version is probably the most familiar and was certainly the one used in the leadership training courses referred to earlier. In essence, this model is 'know yourself, manage your own emotions, be able to understand others and in this way to manage your relationships'.

	Self Personal Competence	Other Social Competence
Recognition	**Self-Awareness** • Emotional self-awareness • Accurate self-assessment • Self-confidence	**Social Awareness** • Empathy • Service orientation • Organisational awareness
Regulation	**Self-Management** • Self-control • Trustworthiness • Conscientiousness • Adaptability • Achievement drive • Initiative	**Relationship Management** • Developing others • Influence • Communication • Conflict management • Leadership • Change catalyst • Building bonds • Teamwork & collaboration

Table 3.0 Table of compentencies (Goleman, 2001, p. 28)

Goleman argued that leaders would inevitably have a high Intelligence Quotient (IQ). It was suggested that organisations are almost self-selecting in this respect, given the demanding and complex nature of their role. Goleman's argument was that intelligence should be considered a given and that it was EI that differentiated the highest-performing leaders. He stated unequivocally:

> Most effective leaders are all alike in one crucial way: they all have a high degree of what has come to be known as Emotional Intelligence. It's not that IQ and technical skills are irrelevant. They do matter, but mainly as 'threshold capabilities'; that is they are the entry-level requirements for executive positions. But my research along with other recent studies, clearly shows that Emotional Intelligence is the sine qua non of leadership. Without it, a person can have the best training in the world, and incisive analytical mind, and an endless supply of smart ideas, but he still won't make a great leader.
>
> (1998, p. 3)

Writing in that same year, Goleman (1998) explored competency models for 181 different positions drawn from 121 companies and organisations worldwide. He noted that their combined workforce numbered millions. He then analysed these competencies in terms of what he considered to be cognitive and those that he deemed to be 'softer skills' which were largely affective in nature. The conclusion was that 67% of the competencies were down the emotional end of the spectrum.

This conclusion was widely disseminated and I still have NCSL PowerPoints and documents from this period, which quote this 67% figure. Of course, the competences, on which Goleman's assertions are based, are by no means equally weighted and this fact alone renders Goleman's conclusion as being questionable. However, Goleman had let the genie out of the bottle and it was certainly not going back in without a struggle. As late as 2008 he was still struggling with the consequences of deploying such a journalistic style and using what was more of a survey than carefully constructed research:

> The subtitle of my 1995 book *Emotional Intelligence* reads, 'Why It Can Matter More Than IQ'. That subtitle, unfortunately, has led to misinterpretations of what I actually say – or at least it seems to among people who read no further than the subtitle. I'm appalled at how many people misread my work and make the preposterous claim, for instance, that 'EQ accounts for 80 per cent of success.'
>
> (2008, p. 1)

Later in that same article he goes on to establish IQ in a much more prominent position than it had been a few years earlier.

> My belief is that if a longitudinal study were done, IQ would be a much stronger predictor than EI of which jobs or professions people can enter. Because IQ stands as a proxy for the cognitive complexity a person can process, it should predict what technical expertise that person can master. Technical expertise, in turn, represents the major set of threshold competencies that determine whether a person can get and keep a job in a given field. IQ, then, plays a sorting function in determining what jobs people can hold. However, having enough cognitive intelligence to hold a given job does not by itself predict whether one will be a star performer or rise to management or leadership positions in one's field.
>
> (2008, p. 1)

Whatever Goleman›s intentions may or may not have been he became the sponsor of a new consultancy and training industry based on EI and one which continues to the present time. Various tests or inventories of emotional competence, intelligence or literacy are available. The aspirant leader who scores poorly in these metrics is usually offered the chance to transform their deficit through a training programme.

Goleman's model is not without its critics. My own critique, offered from a conceptual dimension, would suggest, at least, the following areas of concern:

1. He makes unsupported claims about the power and predictive ability of emotional intelligence.

2. There is an ambiguity in his terminology as he switches between emotional intelligence, emotional literacy and aspects of behaviour and personality. Arguably he never defines his terms, but folds them into his 'catch all' of Emotional intelligence.

3. He argues that he is presenting an innovative understanding. In fact it had already been around for some 20 years.

4. His component-based approach ignores that this is considered by many theorists to be part of the feedback process in transaction models of the communicative process.

5. He has claimed that his ECI-360 test is valid and reliable but this claim lacks consensus amongst other writers and researchers in the field.

Epstein was dismissive of Goleman's claims:

> It has also to be demonstrated that reliable and valid measures of the components can be constructed. Nothing like this has been attempted, and, until it is accomplished, all we have is unsupported speculation about an undefined concept referred to as emotional intelligence.
>
> (Epstein, 1998, p. 19)

If we consider EI from a pragmatic angle and how these competences function then at least two further two significant issues surface. Firstly, Goleman (1996) presents a view of EI that is about having the ability to constrain a challenging panoply of emotions using rational thought. Secondly, it suggests that an alleged EI deficit can be offset by appropriate training.

The mad relative in the attic

Part of the problem of Goleman's model has resulted from his assumption that the cognitive part of our brain should be afforded a dominance. It has already been stated that rational thinking largely resides in the neo cortex whilst emotion is located in the limbic centre. The point was also made that there is a huge disparity in terms of neural processing very much biased towards the limbic centre. For Goleman, his attempt to advise on the impact of EI focuses on our ability or its lack in controlling this unpredictable and intrusive dimension of our thinking:

The ultimate act of personal responsibility at work maybe in taking control of our own state of mind. Moods exert a powerful pull on thought, memory and perception. When we are angry, we more readily remember incidents that support our ire, our thoughts become preoccupied with the object of our anger, irritability so skews our worldview that an otherwise benign comment might now strike us as hostile. Resisting this despotic quality of moods is essential to our ability to work productively.

(Goleman, 1998, p. 83)

Of course, there is much in that quotation which sits comfortably with the progression of this book. However, it is giveaway phrases that he uses such as 'despotic quality' that postulate the limbic centre as being a threat to our effective performance. Writers such as Goleman treat this emotion-generating part of the brain with a degree of suspicion and even fear. In Charlotte Brontë's 1847 novel, *Jane Eyre*, Mr Rochester's insane and unpredictable first wife is kept locked in the attic under supervision of a nurse. Eventually, Bertha escapes, with dire consequences. I find it difficult to read Goleman without *Jane Eyre* running in parallel.

Peters (2012) in his book *The Chimp Paradox* continues in a similar vein. Peters is a psychiatrist based at Sheffield University. He became the resident psychiatrist with Sky Pro Cycling and also with Liverpool FC. He explains the workings of the human brain as having three dimensions: the human, the chimp and the computer. He identifies the 'human' with the frontal lobe of the brain, the area associated with rational thinking. The 'chimp' is offered as a synonym for the limbic centre. The third part, Peters describes as the computer, effectively memory spread through the brain and offering the function as a moderating reference point.

Peters comes from a school of psychological understanding that places a dominance on the role of the cognitive and the rational. The overblown Cognitive Behavioural Therapy approach to psychological problems belongs to this grouping as well. If at this point you would like a diversion from this argument perhaps you might like to Google 'Reasons not to have a chimpanzee as a pet'. This is a quote from one of the results pages:

Aggression is a natural aspect of chimpanzee behaviour and it is not uncommon for chimps to bite each other in the wild. However much a misguided chimp owner continues to love his or her 'child', the chimpanzee will be too dangerous to keep as part of the family. Many owners, to delay the inevitable day that the chimp will have to be removed from the house, will pull the chimp's teeth, put on shock collars – even remove thumbs in the mistaken notion that this will make it impossible for the chimp to climb the drapes.

(Goodall, 2017)

I would suggest that Peters's analogy of the limbic centre as being like a chimp is unhelpful at best and generates a pejorative paradigm at the worst.

This idea of the divided brain, with its components often operating in conflict with each other, has passed into common usage. At the time of writing, *The Guardian* reported on an interview between the BBC reporter, Laura Kuenssberg and the head of the inquiry into the 2003 Iraq war, Sir John Chilcot. Central to the work of this inquiry was the role of then prime minister Tony Blair in sponsoring the conflict. The account notes that:

Sir John Chilcot has said he does not believe Tony Blair was 'straight with the nation' about his decisions in the run-up to the Iraq war.

The chairman of the public inquiry into the 2003 conflict said the former prime minister had however been 'emotionally truthful' in his account of events leading up to the war, meaning he relied on both emotion and fact.

(*The Guardian*, 2017a)

It is strongly suggested that this schizoid view of our brains is inadequate. The following anecdote illustrates the way in which all parts of our brains need to work in a collaborative partnership. Twelve years ago, I was a lead facilitator for NCSL's early headship programme, New Visions. Associated with this role was regular in-house training. In one of these sessions I was with two colleagues who I knew particularly well. It was a day course on advanced facilitation. During the morning break all three of us expressed some uneasiness about the trainer but we could not identify the reason for this. The course was properly structured, the content apposite; but still there was something that just did not add up.

We made it to lunchtime having spent 90 minutes completely distracted from the intended training by this apparent anomaly. Over lunch, one of our trio cracked the problem. He suggested that our trainer had undergone a course of Botox. Leaving aside my personal antipathy towards somebody injecting their face with the most acutely lethal toxin known, it made complete sense. The upper half of the trainer's face was certainly smooth but it was also immobile. Though technically the presentation was acceptable this lack of facial expression, with its negative impact on rapport, was to dismantle the intended learning. Communication needs both content and an emotional frame.

Putting this in a more theoretical frame, this anecdote is about empathy and consequent rapport. If you ask most people to define empathy you will get a response such as 'putting yourself in somebody else's place' or perhaps the more vernacular 'walking in somebody else's shoes'. This is a rather archaic understanding of the nature of empathy. A more contemporary view is that micro-communications (particularly in the faces) of the people we are interacting with are perceived by a network of specialist cells called mirror and spindle cells. Like all information coming to the brain, it is first received by the limbic system and we assess the emotional state of the other.

> Hominoids possess more elaborate control of their facial movements, greater number and complexity of facial expressions and perhaps even a neural basis for emotional representation and comprehension in the form of mirror neurons and spindle cells.
>
> (Parr *et al*, 2005, p. 218)

It is still early days in terms of establishing the neuroscience of social interaction. However, following on from the work on mirror and spindle cells is the discovery of von Economo neurons which again appear to link to social connectivity and which are based in the limbic system. It should be stated that the research into these is still centred around primates and though present in humans, their role has still to be established.

Damassio (1994), a world-class neuroscientist, presents a cogent argument, based on clinical evidence from neural damage, as to the symbiotic nature of reason and emotion in decision-making. Perhaps more strikingly he demonstrates that when there is a pathological disconnect then decision-making is impaired or even incapacitated.

Zeidner *et al* conclude that:

> A growing realization acknowledges that the psychological processes considered to be purely cognitive or intellectual, in fact, de-pend on a synergy between cognition and emotion.
>
> (2002, p. 229)

So perhaps we need to embrace our emotions and celebrate them with the realisation that it is emotions that lift us from existence to life.

The Emotional Intelligence workout

Revisiting the table of competencies (Table 3.0), which summarised the theories presented by Cherniss and Goleman (2001), one that they identified was communication. Of course, a trainer could present ten top tips for effective communication. However, without being able to show how a person-to-person bridge enabled by rapport can be established, effective communication is likely to be strangled at birth. For many trainers and coaches, their fall-back position lies with technicalities and they then struggle to develop these more complex and yet foundational dispositions which transform personal performance from the monochrome to being polychromatic.

In the last decade I not only worked on NCSL's early headship programme, New Visions, but also on other courses such as the London Challenge team programme 'Working Together for Success'. As a result of facilitating these, I worked with at least 500 school leaders. Goleman's model was explored, in many of these courses, when considering aspects of interpersonal leadership. In discussions – and I wish with hindsight that these had been crafted into research – I found no evidence that exposure to the assertions around EI made any discernible difference to the behaviours of these leaders.

Moving beyond anecdote, the research by Zeidner *et al* (2002) conducted a far-reaching critical review of intervention strategies targeted at EI. Their conclusion was that relatively few such programmes could even be considered as EI intervention strategies. They noted that where EI was stated in a given programme's initial aims they were 'surprised and puzzled by the emotional sparseness of such programs' (p. 228). Their review also concluded that many of the interventions used to allegedly enhance emotional competencies/intelligence/literacy were actually based on pre-existing programmes. These were targeted at developing social skills, life-skills, anger management and even health education.

Zeidner *et al* ultimately damn with faint praise when they assert that perhaps the greatest contribution appears 'to reside largely in raising awareness of emotional issues and motivating educators and managers to take emotional issues seriously' (p. 229). A multimillion-pound training and consultancy business is challenged by concluding that:

> Currently, little research shows whether programs touted as EI interventions are actually effective in enhancing the kinds of skills included in current models of EI.
>
> (p. 228).

Grasping the nettle

Leadership is a *smorgasbord* of competences, skills, knowledge and personal dispositions. Ultimately, it must have multiple interactions with a wide range of people and each of these has a context. These never flat line, and even simple transactions can become frontloaded with complex emotions. It is ironic but often the underpinning competencies around these exchanges are called 'soft skills', and yet frequently, they can be bruising, complex and often have unintended outcomes. EI is an attempt to develop a model to secure improved outcomes from such interactions. However, EI as a concept is flawed, it lacks definition, it eludes meaningful measurement and if Zeidner *et al* (2002) are correct it is likely to defy transformation at any meaningful level.

I would suggest three strategies that will strengthen both your personal and professional engagement with others. These do not represent a full EI makeover but will help you become, at least, emotionally presentable!

Give attention to other people; if they feel they are not noticed, if they feel they are not heard or if they are made to feel that you merely want them as an audience, it is unlikely that you will build rapport. I work for University College London and my office is on the sixth floor of the Institute of Education. The exit from the building is on the fourth. I routinely engage others in conversation and establish rapport on that short journey between floors. I consider myself to have failed if we do not exchange good wishes as we get out. Of course, for this to work I have to be intrigued by the other person and be personally authentic. I have done this now for five years. Cynical colleagues have suggested that I am lucky that so far nobody has called security!

When I lecture on the nature and leadership of change sometimes I am asked when you should start initiating a particular change. My answer is: at least a year before you start introducing the change. Change draws on the invested capital of relationships and trust that have been built up over time.

A constant theme of this book is that inappropriate chronic stress is pernicious. Stress is a protective system that has evolved to support short-term action. Characteristically, it moves us into a trance state where our focus is firmly on ourselves and our personal protection; as a result, our options narrow. Often, but not always, other people will have a diminished importance and our personal restraint becomes increasingly unrestrained.

Secondly, commit to the idea that 'calm is strength and stress is weakness'. If we are in a state of physiological stress then this is a poor platform from which to communicate or engage in relationships or to develop strategy. When we are subject to chronic stress, this is driven not only by context but by the state that we have internally generated. We can all too readily reach a position where we begin to view our situation through the spectacles of stress and they are definitely the wrong prescription for effective leadership.

Utilising strategies, which downscale our personal stress such as mindfulness, having a good coach, guided self-review or using the Emotional Freedom Technique (EFT), are not niceties but are part of the staple diet of the effective leader. The approaches will be explored in subsequent chapters.

The third strand, which will support your emotional competence, is to jettison the frenetic. Effective leadership is not assessed by your speed of movement but rather by your ability to keep the orchestra that is the organisation playing in the same key and tempo. Perhaps, Paul Simon nailed it in 'The 59th Street Bridge Song' (Simon and Garfunkel, 1966), where there is a strong recommendation to reduce the pace of life. (Sadly, quoting the exact line from the song would incur substantial cost.) So perhaps to maximise the quotient of our empathy and other emotional competencies we need fewer diagnostics or poorly conceived courses and simply a slower psychological metronome.

4. WHO AM I TO LEAD?

There is a significant amount of literature published on the subject of leadership. Some offer a theoretical travelogue through the landscape of leadership, whilst others, such as Giuliani (2002), the mayor of New York at the time of 9/11, present a more bespoke view.

Crainer and Dearlove (2008) provided a useful guide to the different genres of leadership literature. They argued that:

> Much of the traditional theory falls within three broad categories. Some leadership theories centre on the disposition of the leader, their personality and traits. Others focus on the behaviour of the leader, identifying the different roles they fulfil and preferring to see leadership in terms of what leaders do rather than their characteristics. A third group of theories view leadership as specific to the context.
>
> (2008, p. 3)

It is that first category, that of personal disposition, that is the focus of this chapter. This is probably the dimension of leadership that has been around the longest and it includes trait and personality theories and the politically incorrect 'Great Man Theory'. The latter dates from the 19th century and was popularised by Thomas Carlyle. This term has taken a back seat for some years but has recently resurfaced as a term following the election of Donald Trump (Osimek, 2016). That is offered simply as an observation!

The flawed compass

There are many personality diagnostics being advanced and, just as in the case of EI diagnostics, they are often underwritten by significant commercial investment and substantial marketing.

One of the best-known of these tests is the Myers-Briggs Type Indicator (MBTI). It has been developed, as have a number of other metrics, from the work of psychiatrist, Carl Jung (1875-1961). He advanced the idea of 'introversion' and 'extroversion', together with areas such as 'thinking', 'intuition', 'feeling' and 'sensing'. Jung generated eight theoretical personality types. MBTI has moved the categorisation of personality up to 16 variants. Strangely, many of these tests actually register as learning styles (West-Burnham and Coates, 2005). So, are these diagnostics simply versatile or is their application being stretched for commercial reasons?

Another commonly used derivative from Jung's work is the Insights Discovery Profiling which generates individual outcomes allied to a colour coding. Indeed, many people will recognise the test as soon as you mention, 'It's the one with colours'. The final printout of the Insights Discovery Profile runs to some 23 pages and offers the participant a number of suggestions and an assortment of graphs. Ultimately, it distils its outcomes into four colours: 'fiery red', 'cool blue', 'earth green', and 'sunshine yellow'. The attendant personality styles are summarised as follows:

- FIERY RED – Positive, Affirmative, Bold, Assertive Competitive, Decisive, Strong-willed, Demanding and Task-/Goal-focused

- SUNSHINE YELLOW – Social, Dynamic, Demonstrative, Expressive and Creative

- COOL BLUE – showing no bias, Objective, Detached, Cautious, Analytical, Precise, Questioning and Formal

- EARTH GREEN – Still, Tranquil, Calming, Soothing, Sharing, Patient, Amiable, Caring and Encouraging

This is a very truncated version of 'Insights'. It is popular and certainly on their training days many people express surprise at what the test reveals. Some participants have commented that caveats around stereotyping these different groupings are somewhat thin on the ground. One participant observed that in 100 PowerPoint slides only one related to such a warning (Kelltrill, 2015). The same author also commented that the trainer specified the equality of these different personality types and then proceeded to highlight the 'softer' yellow and green profiles as being less advantageous for leaders and managers. Apparently, even joking, 'There's a yellow in here we need to get rid of her' (Kelltrill, 2015, p. 2). On this particular course, the harder-edged 'fiery reds' and the analytical 'cool blues' were certainly being advocated as being organisationally desirable.

I have just looked at my own Insights Discovery Profile, which was actually administered in 2005. Overall, it is a pretty good summary and I would agree with around 80% of its assertions. I come out as a 'Sunshine Yellow Manager'. Initially, that sounds good and my style of operation is enthusiastic, future-focused, and even inspirational. However, it suggests that I have a tendency towards misplaced optimism, the potential to get bored easily and impatience with people who give significant attention to detail, which is less attractive. I am described as the person who would source the cake for someone's birthday but forget the candles and matches. Time and experience mean that I can work outside my indicated preference. I certainly valued the understanding from the profile but I dislike being corralled as a 'one-trick pony'. The way that Insights Discovery can take root was illustrated from some unrelated research that I was undertaking around the formation and operation of multi-academy trusts. I came across an organisation that was particularly enthusiastic about the Insights Discovery Profiles. All their staff had been tested and their dominant personality type identified together with its associated colour. Subsequently, this attributed colour was included as a band on the bottom of each person's emails. It was explained to me that this would allow staff to communicate more effectively with each other.

Even Insights trainers accept that a significant change in the profile can take place after major life events and also over time. I have come across a number of consultants and organisations that are well entrenched with this diagnostic and its colour-based language has entered their culture and has become part of the defining restricted code of their particular grouping.

MBTI and Insights are underpinned by theoretical constructs which are at least 100 years old. They also tend to assume a relatively steady state of the human mind and this is a triumph of optimism over reality. The Insights Discovery Profile and its 'kissing cousin' MBTI, in my view, offer an inadequate prediction about what happens when a person with a particular personality profile becomes progressively stressed.

There are many other diagnostics that are routinely used such as Hogan, Hogrefe, Cubiks and SHL. Each has its own conceptual basis that defines, for them, how people think and behave. Some test personality; others, competencies such as computation or communication; and yet others identify traits or characteristics. These tests have an appeal in that many are relatively low cost, simple to use and are often online. They also offer the illusion of objectivity. The reality is that such diagnostics are complex and many have issues with reliability and validity. All require interpretation and application to a given context. The inherent complexity of these tests/questionnaires and their potential to impact not only career advancement but also on an individual's self-perception requires a high level of competency in both their administration and subsequent feedback. This is not always the case with some practitioners operating with a somewhat mechanistic approach.

Ready, steady, go

In the early part of the last decade there was a high-impact government initiative, The London Challenge. I ran the team working programme component which was based at The Institute of Education. We worked with the senior leadership teams (SLTs) in 120 secondary schools. This work continued for a number of years after the main initiative ended. At the time, we looked at a number of psychometric tests to try and find one that would help us give feedback to these teams. The best known of these was probably the Belbin Team Role Inventory (BTRI) (Belbin, 1981). This model of teamwork was not really appropriate for our work. The peculiar nature of SLTs means that they certainly have a strategic function where the different skills, perspectives and contributions of each of the team members all play a role. However, Belbin's model understands delivery or the dissemination of the output as being handled by one or two specific individuals. A major function of these school-based teams is that the whole team is required to communicate these outputs and operate 'mob-handed' as cultural change agents.

We eventually selected Motivational Maps. This had been developed by Sale around 2003. He describes them in detail in his book *Mapping Motivation: Unlocking the Key to Employee Energy and Engagement* (2016). They are an amalgam of Maslow, Schein's Career Anchors and the slightly mysterious Enneagram. Though the model has somewhat eclectic origins, we found that it worked extremely well in our consultancy work with teams. Motivational Maps explore motivation and offer three groups of motivators, each with a subset of three. The main groupings are: Work, Relationship and Self. The following table provides a brief summary:

Motivator	Descriptor
Builder (Work)	Seeks money, material satisfactions, above average living
Director	Seeks power, influence, control of people/resources
Expert	Seeks expertise, mastery, specialisation
Friend (Relationship)	Seeks belonging, friendship, fulfilling relationships
Defender	Seeks security, predictability, stability
Star	Seeks recognition, respect, social esteem
Searcher (Self)	Seeks meaning, making a difference, providing worthwhile things
Creator	Seeks innovation, identification with the new ideas, expressing creative potential
Spirit	Seeks freedom, independence, making own decisions

Table 4.0 – Addressing the Motivators (Sale, 2007)

The analysis is undertaken by identifying a given individual's top three motivators and also noting the one they feel is the least influential for them. It began to explain why many members of the teams tended to take up 'set piece' positions and operate from these. Further it often emerged that the team leader – in our work, the head or principal – frequently failed to facilitate the contributions of each member of the team. There was usually an understanding of their wider role in the school but their contribution within the team was frequently less clear. There was also a tendency to see each other as rather homogenous team members rather than as being distinctive personalities with particular contributions. We used the Motivational Mapping process to challenge these perceptions and develop ways of more coherent working.

My eureka moment came when I was working with the SLT of a large comprehensive school in North London. There had been some issues in the team, and on a recent team development residential two members of the SLT had been dismissed in separate incidents for inappropriate behaviour. I carried out the mapping process and tabulated the results (Table 4.1). The highest motivator is number **1**, then **2,** then **3** whilst the lowest is designated **L**.

Motivator/ Role	Builder	Director	Expert	Friend	Defender	Star	Searcher	Creator	Spirit
Principal		3		2	L		1		
VP	L		2				1	3	
VP	L	3	2				1		
AP			2		3	L	1		
AP			L	1	2				3
AP	L						1	3	2
AP			2		3	L	1		
AP	L		1				3	2	
BM	2		1			L	3		

VP – Vice-Principal, AP – Assistant Principal, BM – Business Manager

Table 4.1 The Motivators of the SLT of a North London Secondary School

So, what was it that emerged that was so startling? There were certainly a number of results which were predictable; for example, the high level of the members of the team placing 'searcher' as a key motivator. These, after all, were committed professionals wanting to make a difference in a school situated in a disadvantaged area. The numbers of 'experts', perhaps? Again, this was expected. As SLTs increased in size over the last 15 years or so to meet demands in both capability and capacity, so a number of assistant principals were being appointed to take on specific tasks such as data or pupil achievement. The significant surprise was the very low incidence of the members of the team scoring 'director' as a key motivator. Surely, directing and controlling people and resources was germane to a leadership role?

Having looked closely at the online data generated by the mapping process it was appropriate to explore this issue in greater depth. I then interviewed a sample of the members of these teams individually. The trend indicated by their personal Motivational Map was confirmed: the vast majority did not enjoy interactions with colleagues in terms of persuading, directing their behaviours and instituting processes of accountability. Where there was interaction they admitted that it tended to be from the safe distance of an email. The consequence was that there was relatively little accountability and direction. Wider interviews with staff suggested that they felt a lack of support from some of these teams but did identify individual members of their SLT as being available to support them. Revisiting Table 4.1 for the North London school will show where that support was likely to come from. A further dimension emerged as a result of observing this team in action. They were consummate firefighters, present in significant numbers where there was any incident; but in the process, they tended to emasculate other staff by their lack of professional guidance. Certainly, their interventionist, 'hit and run' approach and lack of narrative leadership failed to communicate the culture that the SLT was trying to develop. In the process, they also placed increasing pressure on themselves.

Over several years I had collected data on a further seven SLTs, all of which were between seven and nine members. The overall sample size was 57. I checked each one of these and there was an evident trend: they were almost copies of each other. It would seem that the aspiration of teaching staff to move into senior leadership and concurrently the selection process had become detached from one of the key functions of the role: that of leading, directing and developing staff.

It is important to note that what was being assessed were motivators and not extant skills. The issue of a given motivator is that it is likely to be where you put your energy and focus. You can engage with other areas but a lack of opportunity to engage in at least some activities which feed your particular motivational set will lower your energy and reduce your job satisfaction. Motivational factors are often explored to support staff performance; it would appear that this aspect of personality has been overlooked in terms of recruitment.

Am I fit to lead?

I was recently seduced by an organisation to undertake a DNA test would help me trace my ancestry. Weeks later, an email arrived that placed me genetically in the North of England and definitely to the east of the Pennines. There was also a suggestion that 15% of my DNA had origins in Ireland. I quite liked the latter, though I am not sure what to do with this intriguing information.

Perhaps I will start celebrating St Patrick's Day to express a resonance with my genetic roots. In a similar way, it is not always clear how the outcomes of personality profiling play out in practice or the potential for the organisations that use them.

Exploring leadership from the perspective of personality, trait or even competency immediately runs into three problems. Firstly, how well is the diagnostic managing to assess its intended area? Secondly, defining leadership has always been problematic; matching trait or personality to its execution is, at least, doubly so. Thirdly, is the diagnostic giving a comprehensive view or is it simply a snapshot of how the person is performing at a particular point in time? These kinds of diagnostics are useful reflectors but all too readily they can become inappropriate constrictors.

One of the prolific writers on psychometric testing is the business psychologist, Mark Parkinson. In an interview, with the *Guardian* journalist Hilary Osborne, he passed a concerned comment on such tests: 'Where they often fail is when people try to use them to assess things that you can't measure, such as creativity or leadership' (Osborne, 2014, p. 1). In this same article there is also the revelation that the disgraced chairman of the Co-operative Bank, the Revd Paul Flowers, was appointed because he did better in psychometric tests than his rivals. Currently, some tests that are now being developed are trying to capture the darker side of people's personalities.

So back to the question that opened this section: 'Am I fit to lead?'. It seems likely that that is the wrong question to ask. In the light of my experience with Motivational Maps, it might be better phrased, 'Do I want to lead?'. It would also be wise to consider this set against the specific context of any particular leadership role.

Returning to the contentious use of psychometric testing, ask yourself, 'Is this a realistic tool to identify me as a leader?'. Arguably, the jury is still out on this. It is suggested that if you enter a selection process with an excessive reliance on psychometric testing without it being backed by appropriate and rigorous interview, a premature departure should be given serious consideration.

5. PEOPLE LIKE ME?

To best deal with unsafe people, we first need to understand what causes us to be unsafe. For the problem is not just outside us; it is inside every one of us.

(Cloud and Townsend, 2017, p. 10)

Human interactions are intricate. They draw on learned behaviours, perceptions of status and role, anxieties and personal disposition. When we are engaged positively, rapport and even affection are established. When they are toxic, harmony moves to cacophony and perhaps rejection. One of the drivers is personal state; again, stress can intervene even to the point of activating the two almond-shaped structures in the limbic centre, the amygdala. Once these are operational, effective communication is unlikely and we move into 'road rage' territory. Focus becomes ever-more self-centred, with an inevitable loss of empathy; normal inhibitions are curtailed and even memory goes. Tyrell (2007) tells of a consultation with a petite lady with an anger problem. Her partner angered her and she moved into an 'amygdala hijack' and threw his mountain bike at him, breaking his leg. So not only is restraint bypassed but our physical responses can move beyond the norm.

Simply difficult

The Canadian psychiatrist, Eric Berne (1978), was fascinated by human interactions. He developed insights into how these operated, developing his theories as 'Transactional Analysis' (TA). The core was that each of us has within us archetypes, a battery of stored resources that we can draw on when we interact socially. One was deemed 'adult', where we are working with others in a state of rational, respectful mutuality. He also invoked the categories of 'adapted child' and 'adapted parent'. The former can involve playfulness and creativity but can also cause us to adopt a dependent stance where we want others to solve our problems. The archetype known as the 'adapted parent' is when we draw on the style of significant others such as parents and teachers. We move to stamp our authority on others and take control. I well remember the horrifying moment when I told one of my children off and heard my father's voice coming from my mouth. TA theory can be particularly helpful in understanding how our interactions are proceeding as leaders and it is also very helpful in coaching conversations where the coach is seeking to establish client autonomy. It can explain the resistance that we can encounter when the other person starts to operate as an 'adapted parent' or dependency when the client moves to the 'adapted child' position. Of course, we would never move to take up either of these positions.

A fascinating spin-off from Berne's work, which provides a useful perspective in understanding the games that people play with us, is Karpman's work (1972). It is usually titled as The Karpman Triangle or more frequently as The Drama Triangle. Perhaps the best synopsis has been provided by Forrest (2008).

The model suggests that in many interpersonal transactions people tend to adopt one of these basic positions:

Victim. This is a position of helplessness and the appeal that they make to others is to request their assistance. This approach to relationships probably has its roots in the person's childhood where such behaviours were used as a means to gain attention. The Victim, if not actually being persecuted, will often seek out a 'persecutor' and also a 'rescuer', that person who will save the day but also perpetuate their victimhood. It has a great deal of resonance with Seligman's (1972) research into Learned Helplessness.

Rescuer. There will be a rush to help people and situations but they can often confirm the other person in a state of dependency. Crucially, by focusing their energy on someone else they can avoid their own issues and personal anxiety. Their actions are all too often disguised as a concern for the victim's needs.

Persecutor. Their response is to project blame and criticism into the situation, often coupled with aggression. There is a strong element of control and authority linked with the position. Perhaps as result of being abused in earlier life, there is a tendency to make a pre-emptive strike.

The Drama Triangle is usually presented as deliberately inverted:

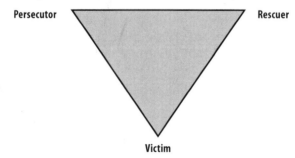

Figure 5.0 The Drama (or Karpman) Triangle

It is a little like a board game. Perhaps like that played in the 1995 film *Jumanji*. The film centres on a board game which rapidly changes from pastime to panic. One of the characters, Alan Parrish, becomes trapped in the game itself. 26 years later in 1995, siblings Judy and Peter Shepherd find the game, begin playing and then unwittingly release the now-adult Alan. The gang resolve to finish the game in order to reverse all of the destruction it has caused. In the Drama Triangle, if someone engages in a dialogue from one of the positions, they are inviting us to join their game. If we accept we can only take up one of the unused positions and, just as in the fictitious board game, Jumanji, we are now trapped in making a series of potentially endless moves. For example, if the other person takes up the 'victim' position we can enter the dialogue as either a 'rescuer' or as a 'persecutor'. The problem begins to emerge when the 'victim' feels unhappy with their role and changes position. If we have been drawn in as the 'rescuer' the only space available to them is that of the 'persecutor' and suddenly our helping response feels as if it is being thrown back in our faces. The positions now begin to rotate round the triangle like some distressing pavane.

Forrest argues that all three positions are in reality expressions of victimhood:

> The three roles on the victim triangle are Persecutor, Rescuer and Victim. Karpman placed these three roles on an inverted triangle and described them as being the three aspects, or faces of victim. No matter where we may start out on the triangle, victim is where we end up, therefore no matter what role we're in on the triangle, we're in victimhood. If we're on the triangle we're living as victims, plain and simple!
>
> (2008, p. 1)

For Forrest, most people have a primary style. She describes this as a 'starting gate', rather like describing our handedness. So, for example, a 'starting gate rescuer' will tend to identify with this role in engaging with another person. However, once on the triangle, the individuals will rotate through the all of the positions, going completely around the triangle, sometimes in a matter of minutes, or even seconds, many times every day.

Forrest goes on to claim:

> I believe that every dysfunctional interaction, in relationship with other or self, takes place on the victim triangle. But until we become conscious of these dynamics, we cannot transform them. And unless we transform them, we cannot move forward on our journey towards re-claiming emotional, mental and spiritual well-being.
>
> (2008, p. 1)

The Drama Triangle provides an analysis of behaviours. Of course, we are not immune from initiating interactions in this way ourselves. However, we are unlikely to get out of this unproductive and often fraught way of conducting relationships unless we know that we are on the triangle. As we become more aware of our own tendencies, we can train ourselves not to join the game when we enter dialogue with others and turn this distracting and draining approach to communications off. We will also recognise when we are being baited to play by others and decline to engage. The colleague who demands action and hints at a problem which you have either created or at one which they think you should have solved can be disarmed with a question as to their responsibility or suggestion or even by a deferred response. They may well move to another position, perhaps that of persecutor, and then spin impotently round the positions. You, meanwhile, have not entered into any 'spur of the moment' commitment to solve the issue and have not been drawn into an unstable discourse.

The dark side

Just over a year ago I underwent radiotherapy for prostate cancer. So far things are looking good. Just as I was about to start my treatment, one of my sons called in to see me and, during the conversation, he asked if I had a CV. I told him that I had one and he asked me for a printed copy. Perceiving this request as being slightly unusual I asked why he wanted it. His reply was somewhat unsettling: 'I thought it would be useful in case I have to do your eulogy'. I suggested to him that pastoral care might not be his forte.

Everybody we know, including those who are close to us, let us down at some point. It may be that they fail to complete something that they promised to do, make an inappropriate comment, perhaps lose their temper because they are tired or stressed. Usually, we can get past these events and move on. The problem becomes challenging when the issue changes from being about something to being about someone, when we find that it is not a specific failure or encounter that is causing us unease but a particular individual leaving us feeling concerned, anxious, edgy, tentative and apprehensive. It may be, in a professional context, that the person makes an exemplary contribution and is not prone to irritating gaffes and mistakes but still leaves us feeling wary. This section explores our interaction with such people and why they can often be categorised as unsafe.

It is important to differentiate between those people we do not find interesting and those people we perceive as presenting some kind of threat towards us. In general, we tend to like people who are like us or like people who we would like to be like. The adage that 'opposites attract' really does not gain much traction. Recently, I went to a party and had a conversation with someone I have known for many years. They proceeded to recount to me the role of Mosquito fighter-bombers in the North Atlantic in World War Two. After 20 minutes, I was certainly beginning to lose the will to live and had accumulated more knowledge on the subject than I either needed or wanted. However, this somewhat focused individual, while scoring highly on the boredom index, could not be described as being unsafe. Conversely, I was introduced to someone at work and I experienced a powerful antipathy towards them. Superficially, they presented as being pleasant and engaging and yet all the time I was in conversation with them, alarm bells were ringing in my head. I had a strong desire to end the conversation and move from the room. Working with them later, I realised that this feeling of unease, was a precursor to a somewhat tense professional relationship. Our feelings in such circumstances are not foolproof, but equally, failing to give them attention because we are struggling to find a rational basis for our concerns is not wise either.

Before unpacking this idea of safe and unsafe people, a caveat should be offered. Human beings are wonderfully rich and frequently behave in ways that cannot be contained in a box. Over-analysing and categorising people has the potential to do them a serious injustice. I find that people are surprising, hard to define and that they often exceed my beliefs in either their potential or kindness. People, also, tend to emphasise different parts of their personalities when under (dis)stress, rather like a low tide exposing rocks on the coastline.

Even allowing for the above reservations, people do exhibit personality types which can be problematic. The Harvard psychologist Michael Macoby (2001) suggested that there were three main types of personalities: erotic, obsessive and narcissistic. These are derived from Freud's work. However, even allowing for that, they could be better phrased. Certainly, two of them would be perceived as insulting and one, the erotic, comes out, at best, as being ambiguous. A less contentious labelling might be to understand them as follows:

Erotic. This where the individual's focus is very much on **relationships**. They are likely to prioritise harmony.

Obsessive: Here the focus is on **detail and system**. For a person with such a slant, 'near enough' is unlikely to be good enough.

Narcissistic: The world is understood in terms of themselves. Almost certainly they will have a clarity of **vision**. The importance of achieving their personal goals can drive an organisation forward, though this can require their personal agenda and that of the organisation to become synonyms.

Most leaders would find a synthesis of all three elements to be beneficial. However, if any one of these types is exaggerated, there are likely to be negative consequences. The 'erotic' will major on the relational aspects of the organisation but find decision-making challenging because someone may not like the outcome which could hurt someone. The 'obsessive' will try and make people fit the system, leading to those around feeling disenfranchised. The 'narcissist' can only really thrive when they are fuelled by the admiration of others.

Recently, I listed people who have caused me significant problems in the last 25 years. It was an interesting exercise and generated a 'top ten'. Against their names I noted the behaviours that had caused me concern and even distress and distilled these into a list of five:

- Poor listeners
- Lack of empathy
- Ruthless in order to place themselves in the pole position, often at my expense
- A tendency to steal my ideas and my recognition by others
- Considerable difficulty in receiving any criticism/feedback

In shorthand terms, however affable they may be, everything is always about them and, drawing on Macoby's terminology, they are narcissists.

I would suggest that the defining trait of the narcissist is the lack of empathy. Peck (1988) recounts a clinical interview with a 15-year-old, Bobby, after his older brother had committed suicide. Not surprisingly, Bobby found it difficult to discuss the tragic event. In an attempt to establish rapport, Peck asked him what he had been given for Christmas. Bobby replied that his parents had given him a .22 rifle. It transpired that it was not a new one but actually the gun that his brother had used to commit suicide.

Peck called the parents in the following day. In the conversation that ensued, they could not even get close to understanding why this might not be the gift of choice for their younger son. The father even commented:

> We couldn't afford to get him a new gun. I don't know why you are picking on us. We gave him the best present we could. Money doesn't grow on trees, you know. We're just ordinary working people. We could have sold the gun and made money. But we didn't. We kept it so we could give Bobby a good present.

> (1988, p. 63)

Narcissists, though sharing a number of defining traits, are not a completely homogeneous group. Goleman (2006) divides them into three, his so-called 'Dark Triad': the narcissist, the Machiavellian and the psychopath. Whilst the latter form a fascinating group who are more often associated with the more lurid acts of criminality, it is the first two that are of interest in our context.

There is often the distinction made between healthy and unhealthy narcissists. It is argued that the healthy narcissist has that overarching ambition and drive, tempered by some self-reflection and an openness to reality checks, whilst the unhealthy narcissist craves admiration more than love. Experience would suggest that this division is flawed, and though there may be a spectrum ranging from 'narcissism light' to 'self-aggrandisement central', stress may well have a role to play in the person traversing the spectrum. Surprisingly, it is when the narcissist is achieving success that their faults become even more pronounced. The opiate of success shuts them off from challenge and advice and they become increasing risk-takers. Under pressure, they can become ever-more vindictive, attributing blame to subordinates in an attempt to mitigate judgement being made on them. (John, the assistant vice-principal from Chapter 2, would illustrate this kind of personality type.)

Goleman's second category, the Machiavellian or 'Mach' is named after Niccolo Machiavelli for his book *The Prince* (1985). The basic assertion of the treatise is that self-interest is the sole driving force in human nature and that altruism has no role to play. Whilst the 'Mach' see others as pawns or interchangeable components to be manipulated to achieve his or her own ends, they remain more realistic about themselves and others and the edge is taken off the narcissistic aggrandisement. (In Chapter 2, Fiona (the vice-principal) would probably best characterise this personality type.)

The 'Mach' is described by Goleman as having 'tunnel vision empathy: they can bring someone's emotions into focus mainly when they wish to use that person for their own ends' (2006, p. 126). Whereas the narcissist has a casual disregard for others, the Mach can play the system for their own ends and display a selective capacity to understand what someone might be thinking in a way that is best described as social cunning. I have a friend who is a Machiavellian. It took me a long time to understand that their proffered concern was shallow and that any information that I shared was a currency that would be traded for their benefit.

Most people know somebody who displays these traits; many will have worked for people who are narcissists. The actual numbers within the general population is not very clear. Generally, it is estimated between 6% and 10% fall into this category, with a higher representation of men. It is not just likely that you will come across them but inevitable. In the last decade in English schools there has been a move towards collaboration and an advocacy of distributed leadership. Since the changes brought in under Michael Gove (Secretary of State for Education 2010-2014), significant changes were made to English schools. The role of local authorities in education was diminished or in many areas virtually ended. In their place, a number of quasi-autonomous aggregations have grown up, with multi-academy trusts coming to the fore. This time of transition to new structures requires a hard-edged leadership that can drive both standards and structures simultaneously. This is fertile ground for the narcissistic leader where time pressures do not facilitate discussion and where there is scope for personal glory beyond that possible in headship.

In interviews, the narcissist will often shine, giving their personal guarantee for the solution of complex problems. They are often charismatic and visionary, providing hope for a beleaguered organisation. However, the vision subscribed to is theirs and theirs alone. The healthy narcissist may well drive things forward; if, however, the appointee is an unhealthy narcissist or, indeed, a more constructive one that begins to come under high levels of stress, then their leadership team will crumble within a short space of time.

Several years ago, I did some consultancy work for a school where the head was almost certainly a narcissist. He had a narrow vision for education seen only in terms of GCSE grades. Staff rooms were disbanded and replaced with coffee points which did not allow cells of dissension to develop. He replaced his senior leadership team with what could only be described as bouncers. Any member of staff who expressed dissent or criticism would receive photocopies of alternative jobs from the *TES* in their pigeonholes within the week. Apart from school and results, the only other thing that he would discuss was his cat. I could not get the image of Ernst Stavro Blofeld out of my mind.

Narcissists cannot be considered safe people to work for or indeed with. If your boss is a narcissist then it is probably best to hold your job lightly and keep a way out in view. Always sympathise with his/her feelings but expect nothing back in return. If your opinion is sought remember that it is information that will solve a problem that is being sought and not an opinion about them personally.

It is also good to develop your time-management skills because more will be asked of you than either your capability or capacity can feed. You will be required to share ideas but expect to see them rebadged as theirs. If a course of action is being suggested that hints at becoming apocalyptic, suggest an alternative that will put them in a better light. Do not expect the person to change significantly. That is not to say that it cannot happen, but recognise that it is not the most likely scenario.

The curious incident of the dog with its teeth in my leg

Some years ago, I had friends who had a Rhodesian Ridgeback. Whenever I went to see them, it used to bite me. A bite of passage? The owners said it was just being friendly. I was less convinced and subsequently found other friends and a less challenging social life.

Over the years, I have come across the human equivalents of this Ridgeback. They have cropped up in many different areas of life: social, work situations and, oh yes, church as well. Somehow, these people have had little concern for my wellbeing, cared little if they caused me pain. Being around them left me feeling perpetually uneasy. It was a slight (but only a slight) relief to find that they did the same to others. There was only their agenda and people were viewed more as commodities. They often displayed self-aggrandisement and certainly had the empathy of a concrete block.

These individuals or narcissists, to give them their correct name, are unsafe people. Therapists have recorded that they see very few of these people for consultation but do, however, see a number of people who have had dealings with them. Narcissists have very low levels of self-awareness and simply do not have regret at what they do to others, nor do they usually grasp the need for personal reform.

6. THE PRIMACY OF TRUST

Be yourself. Everyone else is already taken.

(Oscar Wilde)

Julie had been appointed as acting vice-principal during the interregnum before Robert took up the post as principal. The governing body were keen that her post should be ratified. Robert capitulated to their wishes. Julie was dyslexic, and with appropriate support and strategies this should not have precluded her from the role. In practice, her approach was to operate from a stance of denial that she had any issues. Part of the portfolio of her role was parental partnership. A relatively minor subset was organising parent consultations. The first of these became problematic when she notified the parents of one start time and the staff a start time 30 minutes later. The error was compounded when she sought to shift the blame to an administrative assistant and then cover her tracks by lying. This became established as her signature behaviour. Administrative errors linked to her learning difficulty would occur and then she would try to relocate the blame with others and then lie to cover her tracks. This soon caused staff to question her competency and, more importantly, eroded the more ephemeral dimension of trust. Robert, meanwhile, was left with another problem in his already overflowing inbox.

There have been a number of studies that emphasise the importance of trust. Comer *et al* (1996) undertook research that demonstrated the link between schools and their embedded community and showed that strengthening the connections in urban schools between education professionals and parents in disadvantaged areas, as well as building trust with stakeholders, can raise achievement. Louis and Kruse (1995) explored trust from a similar stance, again with an emphasis on schools in an urban context. Meier (1995) argues that building trust among teachers, school leaders, students, and parents was a key component of the success of a middle school that she developed in Harlem.

Less explicit in much of this research is an explanation of the nature of trust. When we say that we trust someone, it really is quite complex and certainly engages both the cognitive and also the more intuitive areas of the brain. When I say that I trust my dentist, my focus is on his/her professional competencies. However, when I say that I trust my wife, that is an altogether more elaborate understanding of trust. In order to engage with trust there is an evident need for a more concise working definition. It is not sufficient to see trust as the organisational equivalent of owning a Labrador.

One of the most foundational pieces of educational research on trust is that of Bryck and Schneider (2002). They conducted nearly a decade of case studies in more than 400 Chicago elementary schools. This was a significant piece of research when you consider that they spent over four years in 12 particular school communities, observing classroom instruction and talking to teachers about the progress and problems in their reform efforts. Periodic surveys of teachers, principals, and students were also collated. They looked at the changing relational dynamics in all Chicago elementary schools over a six-year period. Trends in individual numeracy and literacy were explored to assess the value that each school was adding to student learning and the extent to which this was improving over time. They correlated changes in academic productivity with their survey results on school trust. Their conclusion was that trust makes a major contribution to school reform. From this extraordinary longitudinal research has emerged a model for understanding trust.

Vodicka (2006) provides useful secondary analysis of Bryck and Schneider (2002), as well as analysis of a number of other writers such as Tschannen-Moran and Hoy (2000), distilling their work into four components:

- **Competence:** Bryck & Schneider (2002, p. 24) spoke of this being the 'execution of an individual's role responsibilities'. The continuous demonstration of competence can appear challenging, particularly in the complex and developing context of contemporary education. There is an inter-dependent relationship between the leader and the led which relies on performance and the execution of each of their respective roles. In the context of accountability, producing results is often seen as the best determinant of competence (Shaw, 1997).

- **Consistency:** When leaders tackle culture, whether to dismantle dysfunctional culture or to sponsor the evolution of a more appropriate culture that supports its aims, consistency must be pre-eminent. Schein (2010) argues that:

> The most powerful mechanisms that founders and leaders, managers and parents have available for communicating what they believe in or care about is what they systematically pay attention to. This can mean anything from what they notice and comment on to what they can measure, control, reward and in other ways deal with systematically. Even casual remarks and

questions that are geared to a certain area can be as potent as
formal control mechanisms and measurements.

(p. 237)

It is hard to sail when the wind keeps abruptly changing direction.

- **Compassion:** We all want to believe that we matter and that we
are noticed. Compassion is about care which in turn is the centre
of a trusting relationship. If you respond to an individual with
indifference then they are unlikely to commit to your intentions.
In a relationship, compassion suggests that there is also some level
of protection being offered, that the leader has your back. It can
be demonstrated by recognising the contributions of members of
the organisation. A smile, a comment or an enquiry all help build
compassion. Remembering some basic facts about the individual will
turn up the thermostat of the relationship with the proviso that your
comment or enquiry is authentic.

- **Communication:** Underpinning good communication is rapport,
a connectedness which comes from a melee of language, body
language and tonality. I was coaching a senior leader who could not
comprehend why their communications regularly became mired in
resentment. After all, what was being said was simply common sense.
Over several sessions it became clear that the leader viewed others as
a receptacle for their ideas, their communication was all push and no
pull. There is always a second conversation taking place between the
subconscious minds of the interlocutors. Time spent listening is never
wasted, as the other person verbally engages with the concepts that
you are trying to get across. Leaders are often involved in constructing
and implementing change; in many instances, moving the reluctant
to new realities. All such change should have started long before the
idea was even thought of, preferably years before. Its reception will be
enhanced by all those comments you have made, enquiries into their
circumstances, the times when you took an interest in their wellbeing
and even the times when you simply smiled at them.

There was a great television programme entitled *Faking It*, which ran on
Channel 4 from 2000-2004. Unlikely individuals received rudimentary training
in various professions to pass themselves off as the real thing. It included
cellist Sian Evans learning to be a club DJ, burger-van proprietor Ed Devlin
training with Gordon Ramsay to become a *cordon bleu* chef, and a former naval
petty officer being trained as a drag artist. In many ways, these were echoes

of *Pygmalion* by George Bernard Shaw (1916). It was fascinating to see these individuals transcend their normal personae.

If Bryck and Schneider (2002) are correct and a series of corner stones are needed to build trust, then can they be 'faked'? This is unlikely: leadership is not an edited television show or a stage play; it is very much about the long haul in a context where actions and interactions receive both informal scrutiny and structured audit.

The pivotal role occupied by trust connects with the emergent theory around Authentic Leadership. As a leadership theory, it has its roots in the 1960s, but has received some impetus from the ex-Medtronic CEO, now Harvard Academic, Bill George (2003). Although Authentic Leadership has not been fully articulated, there is consensus that it identifies with these distinct qualities:

- **Self-awareness:** The leader reflects on her/his strengths and weaknesses and values.

- **Relational transparency:** There is an open sharing of ideas, thinking, beliefs and values. The leader is not emotionally impulsive and does not 'splurge' these across colleagues.

- **Balanced processing:** The perspectives and contributions of colleagues are sought, as is the augmentation and challenge to their own thinking.

- **Internalised moral perspective:** The leader has a carefully constructed and internalised moral purpose. This is consistent but not rigid to the point of bigotry.

So, there would seem to be some connection with the conclusions of Bryck and Schneider (2002) and Authentic Leadership. Perhaps in the end Oscar Wilde got there first with the opening quote to the chapter!

Stress testing

This chapter argues for the imperative of the leader building trust. This is through carefully maintaining a focus on their own indices of trust. Research evidence suggests that these are not simply niceties but are germane to both leading the organisation and also in the very achievement of student success. Developing personal qualities that support trust is not formulaic but comes from self-awareness and reflection, perhaps by yourself or with the support of a coach.

The core theme of *It's Doing My Head In* is exploring the impact of stress on impairing effective leadership. Each of the suggested four trust builders

– competency, communication, consistency and compassion – are highly susceptible to being downgraded by stress. Taking them in turn:

- **Competence:** There are many studies that relate to the deterioration of performance as stress levels rise, such as Nixon (1976). Nixon picks up on Selye (1956) and his idea of 'eustress' and 'distress', positive and negative stress.

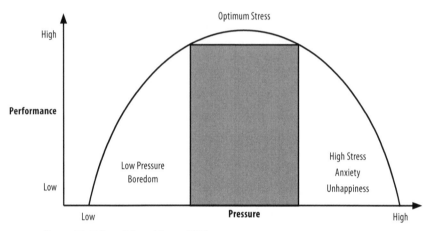

Figure 6.0 (Adapted from Nixon, 1976)

Following the inverted U-curve, as stress builds, so does performance, until a tipping point is reached and then performance starts to decline with increasing severity. Research has shown this to hold true for a wide range of human activity and this certainly includes cognition.

Stress will affect our ability to remember, to process new information and then to apply these to analysis and decision-making. Mental exhaustion brought on by a total package of stress – that is, the sum of the stress at work and from events in our personal lives – will result in us being less able to concentrate and also more likely to make significant mistakes.

- **Consistency:** Stress engenders a sense of the immediate as it is intended to do with an extreme focus on the now. We react to the present situation or crisis and lose both our perspective of the wider context of our actions and our connection with the strategic long game.

- **Compassion:** The point has been made that when we become stressed, our focus changes; we move to become the centre of our world. When we are inappropriately stressed, we increasingly dismiss other people to the periphery of our concerns.

- **Communication:** Negative stress has the potential to impair communication. The impact of this stress can trigger a whole host of responses that will inhibit communication. When we are stressed, the stressors will preoccupy our thoughts and make it difficult to sustain coherent dialogue. Part of our compensatory mechanism might be to concentrate on each word in an effort to speak clearly. In turn, this will damage the natural flow of our speech and this will certainly be picked up by anyone speaking with us and cause a sense of unease. Stress is linked to being prepared to act in the face of a threat. Many automatic actions are taken over as a result and this can affect the fluidity of the movement of our tongue, making our speech sound slurred. Stress will also make us reinterpret the actions of others and become suspicious and even paranoid.

As your stress increases, it is certain that the trust others have in us will begin to ebb. Over time, we may have banked considerable amounts of trust with our colleagues. In times of organisational recession these savings can become rapidly depleted.

Jerry-built

Organisations simply cannot be built on a trust deficit. Writing in the more specific context of teams, Lencioni (2002) argues that trust is foundational for these to function:

> Teams that lack trust waste inordinate amounts of time and energy managing their behaviours and interactions within the group. They tend to dread team meetings, and are reluctant to take risks in asking for or offering assistance to others. As a result, morale on distrusting teams is usually quite low, and unwanted turnover is high.
>
> (2002, p. 196)

On the next page is his summary of the inverted cascade of consequences that flow from the absence of trust:

Figure 6.1 The five dysfunctions of a team (Lencioni, 2002, p. 188)

For Lencioni:

> In the context of building a team, trust is the confidence among team members that their peers' intentions are good and that there is no reason to be protective or careful around the group. In essence team members must get comfortable being vulnerable with one another.
>
> (2002, p. 195)

These five potential dysfunctions are not distinct but form an interlocked, coherent whole. The absence of trust means that team members do not share openly through fear of conflict. This means that insights from some members are withheld and that appropriate challenge is not offered, which could take contributions to another level. Subsequently, the political infighting robs the team of its efficacy and dissipates its energy.

Of course, as we lead organisations, people have to consider the level of trust that they afford to us; and in a similar way, we have to evaluate how much we can trust our colleagues. If we cannot trust our colleagues, we are likely to increase our monitoring of their work and behaviours. This is legitimate where someone is moving in to a new role and we are their line manager. If they are an established post holder, such extensive monitoring is less legitimate and will be costly to us. Such a person will take a piece of our attention or what we might call our headspace. It is unwise to accept this and we should make it clear that the situation cannot continue. Communication, consistency and areas of competency can all be developed. However, enhancing compassion or redefining moral purpose in another person presents a significant challenge. There is a role here for coaching the person or we may need to summon the courage and resolve to remove them from their current role.

7. IT'S DOING MY PRINCIPLES IN

If the soul is left in darkness, sins will be committed. The guilty one is
not he who commits the sin, but he who causes the darkness.
(Bishop Myriel, *Les Misérables*, Hugo, 2002)

For over a decade, pupils in state schools in Atlanta, Georgia, appeared to
make significant progress. The main evidence for this came from mandated
standardised tests, Criterion Referenced Competency Tests (CRCT). These
gains generated considerable interest and earned the Area Superintendent,
Beverly Hall, personal acclaim. In 2009 the American Association of School
Administrators named her national superintendent of the year.

Eventually, questions began to be asked about the improbability of the
scale of these improvements being rooted entirely within strategies for
raising educational achievement. In 2009, faced with persistent rumours of
malpractice, the state governor ordered an enquiry. From this point onwards,
the wheels came off. The investigation estimated that, in that year alone, 44 out
of 56 of the Atlanta public schools had cheated in the CRCT assessments. The
fallout was huge, with 11 teachers either receiving custodial sentences or large
fines. Dr Hall was charged with racketeering, theft, influencing witnesses and
conspiracy. She died of cancer before she was brought to trial.

Similar investigations have taken place in other countries. In the UK, *Guardian*
journalist Warwick Mansell (2015) cited statistics which had been published the
previous year by the exams regulator, Ofqual, showing a 61% rise in the number
of schools and colleges where there were concerns relating to malpractice over
that year, with 217 penalty notices being issued. That is one for every 30 schools
or colleges in the UK. The *Guardian* newspaper had submitted freedom of
information requests to Ofqual. The responses identified two schools by name,
whilst the overwhelming majority were described in a generalised manner and
their anonymity was preserved.

Over the last two years, I have coached eight middle and senior school leaders
who have been involved in examination fraud. One example was sending an
empty .zip file to an examining board to buy time by creating an apparent
administrative delay. Another involved a head of department being instructed
to take her team to another school within the same academy chain to re-order

pupil assessment portfolios. These were BTEC science submissions for Year 11 pupils. The team went over evening after evening. The term 're-order' was undoubtedly a euphemism for something much more substantial.

Men (and women) behaving badly

Two strong messages emerged from coaching these clients. Firstly, I had not stumbled across a conspiracy of evil or a tranche of narcissists with a tenuous grasp of moral purpose. These people, with one exception, were committed professionals and also thoroughly pleasant individuals. In other circumstances, I would have enjoyed socialising with them and certainly would have been very happy for them to teach my own children. The second message to emerge was that they all displayed a sense of bewilderment. They could not understand how their personal moral compass had swung so wildly.

A discussion with most people will reveal that they believe they hold a largely non-negotiable core of personal values from which their behaviours are advanced. They will usually admit that they sometimes fall below their optimal standards but these values or moral principles are still held to be of great importance to them. They have come to a position on what is acceptable and unacceptable.

We often talk about personality and character. The former is frequently cast as a touch of nature and a touch of nurture. Character is more generally understood as relating to our moral stance. It is often perceived as being forged in the white heat of significant experiences, reflection, philosophy, the inputs from family and religious belief. Exploring various strands of research suggests that such beliefs are not always as stable as we might like to think. The pun used as a chapter heading is intended to capture something of this malleability.

Let us start with a trip down memory lane. In 1961, psychologist Stanley Milgram conducted a series of experiments to determine the impact of authority figures on the behaviour of others. A major motivation for conducting these experiments had come in the wake of wartime atrocities, notably the Holocaust, and an examination of the defences that were used by the perpetrators that they were 'only obeying orders'.

Forty volunteers were recruited. They were grouped with a white-coated technician and a 'learner' whilst they were manipulated into taking the role of the 'teacher'. The teacher was shown an adjacent room with what appeared to be an electric chair. They were told to administer electric shocks to the learner and informed that these would escalate if wrong answers were given; but they were reassured that the voltage administered would remain within safe limits.

Before the experiment began they sampled the level of what was a relatively mild electric shock. The learner was then strapped into the chair and the teacher taken to the adjacent room with the technician. They could communicate with, but could not see, the learner. In front of the teacher was a dial indicating the level of shock they could administer for wrong answers to the questions that they were given to ask. The shock generator was calibrated in 15-volt intervals, with a warning not to exceed 450 volts. Before starting, mention was made of the fact that the learner had a heart condition. In reality, shocks were not actually given to the learner, who merely simulated distress.

As the voltage was raised in response to more and more wrong answers, the learner began in to display distress. Most of the teachers appealed to the technician to stop. Some of the teachers wanted to withdraw and even repay the fee they had been given to participate in the experiment. At this point, the technician gave a series of four escalating instructions:

1. Please *continue*.

2. The experiment requires that you *continue*.

3. It is absolutely essential that you *continue*.

4. You have no other choice, you *must* go on.

If they still questioned the experiment after these instructions, they were allowed to stop. Remember, the 'learner' was an actor simulating pain and distress.

Pre-experimental predictions of the numbers of participants who would raise the level of shock to a lethal 450 volts were between 0% and 3%. The actual outcome from the experiment showed that 65% (26/40) of the volunteers were prepared, albeit unwillingly in a number of cases, to administer damaging levels of electrical shock.

The major conclusion reached was that people are susceptible to the instructions given by an authority figure, in this case, the technician. However, there was also evidence of distress to the volunteer teachers when levels of coercion were applied. It does seem that excessively assertive leadership has the potential to override our moral boundaries. Later in the chapter, I want to draw parallels between the damage done to individuals through such experiments and the imposed moral override on staff.

Off their trolley

Fast forward 46 years and a team headed up by psychologist Joshua Greene (in Paxton et al, 2007) researched moral decision-making. They used scenarios such as the infamous trolley problem. A situation is described where a trolley is racing down the railway tracks towards five people who are tied up; if unchecked, it would kill them. Participants were asked to imagine that they were standing on a bridge under which the trolley will pass. Next to them is a very large man. If they were to push him off the bridge, an act which would kill him, then the trolley could be stopped and the five captives saved. So, the question is posed as to whether they should push the man off the bridge or not.

From this work, Greene and his team (in Paxton *et al,* 2007) advanced a dual process theory of moral judgement. They argued that the brain has two competing moral subsystems:

1. **Emotional,** intuitive so-called deontological judgements (*eg,* don't push the fat man off the footbridge in the trolley problem).

2. **Rational,** calculated, utilitarian judgements (*eg,* push the fat man off to save more lives in total).

Subsequent experimental work used cognitively based pre-tasks to tilt the moral processing towards one of these systems or the other (Paxton *et al,* 2012). Such tasks appeared to cause participants to move towards the more utilitarian or rational response. The conclusion reached was that increasing the 'cognitive load' as a more utilitarian approach was adopted slowed down the making of moral decisions.

Greene (in Paxton *et al,* 2007) provides a useful insight into moral decision-making coming from either a more rational or a more emotional basis. However, I am not convinced that his study sheds a significant amount of light on the apparent moral fragility of the clients that I have been working with or indeed on some of those involved in the Atlanta Testing Scandal. In Greene's research, there seems to be little consideration given as to whether the stress that the participants were suffering was acute or chronic. All the people that I have worked with relating to examination fraud or with other ethical lapses were all mired in long-term, chronic stress. It is suggested that this was a significant factor when they made decisions, and, in a number of cases, decisions that they were later to regret.

Countdown
Another piece of research that provides an interesting insight into the moral choices that we make and how these choices can relate to our value system was carried out by Darley and Batson (1973).

This was undertaken at Princeton Theological Seminary with students preparing to undertake pastoral work within churches. A group of 40 students were taken to a holding room and one group were asked to prepare a talk on the parable of 'The Good Samaritan', the other on the less morally charged subject of seminary jobs. Individually, they were sent to deliver their talk in the assessment hall, a short walk away. As they were sent, they were instructed with various levels of urgency. Essentially, you have plenty of time to get there or you need to hurry.

Between the two buildings was an actor feigning what could be interpreted as ill health or perhaps drunkenness. Observers noted down the responses of the students on their way to their assessment. Some stopped and helped, others reported the man's plight when they got to the assessment centre and others merely hurried past the man.

Before the research was undertaken, one hypothesis was that students who had reflected on that quintessential story of helping someone in distress would be more likely to render assistance. The surprising findings were that the subject that the students had prepared for their talk produced no significant difference in their response to the man in distress. What did appear to influence the help given was the urgency (or its lack) with which they had been dispatched from the holding room. This research seems to indicate that moral action can be curtailed or facilitated by time pressure.

Immoral afternoons

Research by Gunia *et al* (2014) argued that there is a moral downturn as a day wears on. They attributed this to the effect of circadian rhythms. They also suggested that a further contribution to this was made by our chronotype, *ie* whether you are a lark or an owl: an early riser or a late night person.

I have been intrigued by the research published by Kouchaki and Smith (2014). They also suggest that time of day does influence our moral decisions. Their research suggests an altogether simpler explanation in that the normal, unremarkable experiences associated with everyday living can deplete an individual's capacity to resist moral temptations as the day wears on.

There is no suggestion here that at midday you have *carte blanche* to open the gin bottle or clandestinely pop down the local betting shop. Actually, I could cite cases where this has happened; however, that might be a subsequent book for a different audience! Both sets of researchers do agree that we are more vulnerable to moral variation in the afternoon.

Revenge is sweet

Danziger, Levav and Avanaim-Pesso (2011) researched the work of judges considering parole applications in Israel. It soon emerged that judgments that were more favourable to the applicants were more likely first thing in the morning and immediately after lunch. Just before lunch and towards the end of the afternoon the decisions made were more likely to go against the applicant.

The decision-making process was mapped against the blood sugar levels of the judges. There was a clear correlation between imposing negative judgements and low blood sugar levels. I am sure that the intention of the judicial system was to arrive at objective conclusions, but it must be disturbing both to the judges and to the applicants that their potential freedom could be significantly influenced by the physiological state of the bench. Of course, there are wider implications for all involved in making decisions, not just the judiciary.

Disgusting!

This final piece of research by Pizarro, Inbar and Helion (2011) focuses on the impact of that powerful emotion such as disgust can have on a participant's viewpoint. In this paper, and also in an engaging summary delivered as a TED talk (2013), Pizarro and his colleagues argue for the importance of our feelings of disgust and suggests they are a key survival mechanism. If we are disgusted with a sight or smell, we tend to recoil from the source and so avoid something that is potentially harmful. Working at Cornell University, they devised a test for levels of disgust. It was found that there was a spectrum of intensity of feeling in this area within the population. They also correlated the intensity with which disgust was felt from a moral viewpoint. It was concluded that the greater the intensity with which a person felt disgusted, the more conservative his or her views were likely to be. An individual who was identified as having lower levels of intensity of feeling disgusted was more likely to demonstrate a more liberal stance.

On a roll, they interviewed people about their political views and for one of the groups interviewed they placed a dispenser of hand sanitiser next to the questionnaire. This was held to remind participants of the presence of disgust. The group that completed questionnaires adjacent to the hand sanitiser demonstrated a distinct ideological movement to the right when contrasted with the control group. I find Pizarro's work both entertaining and at the same time quite disturbing. It suggests that yet again our inviolate moral principles can be all too easily corrupted.

I am writing this chapter shortly after the election of Donald Trump as US President. Trump, somewhat of an enigma, is certainly to the political right. My somewhat tangential nightmare is that he could have been elected as a result of voters being exposed to hand sanitiser and possibly roadkill. However, maybe that is a hypothesis too far.

Conclusion

The preceding catalogue of psychological insights into moral choices may seem rather confusing and a touch random. Is the message, 'Do not make decisions with a strong moral component whilst standing on a bridge accompanied by a white-coated technician who is clutching a bottle of hand sanitiser – and definitely avoid afternoons'? Probably not!

There are some pointers that can be gleaned from these strands of research, and these could help prevent poor morally based decisions being made with dream-haunting consequences. Crucially, we should recognise that we are not moral bulwarks but rather fallible human beings. Our moral compass can have a propensity to swing and it can be thrown out of kilter by the lodestone of circumstances and personal state. Understanding this and building safeguards into our moral agency can be very effective.

The repetitive message of this book is that sustained stress is not only uncomfortable and harmful; it also changes the way we think. On becoming stressed, our focus will tend to change from embracing a wide range of options considered from multiple viewpoints to a largely self– directed mono-focus. When stressed, we will tend to make decisions for the now, and these will be disconnected from our wider context. We may, for example, be extremely critical and judgemental of a subordinate and use our status to humiliate them. This may feel apposite where someone has made a significant mistake. However, a stress-driven castigation may rob the long game of that person's loyalty. So, the more we can make our moral decisions from a stance of calm, the more considered they are likely to be and the more connected to the wider functioning of the organisation.

A significant skill that can help to offset our swinging moral compass is the practice of employing the 'observational self': learning how to view ourselves almost as if we were another person. In doing this, we begin to put to one side the persona that we try to present to others, suspend negative feelings that we may have about ourselves and reduce self-justifying position-taking.

It is a myth to assume that we can determine our own behaviours – or even perhaps assess our decisions – better than others. We readily assume that we can judge and predict our own behaviours better than non-involved strangers can, but the research doesn't bear this out. Nisbett and Wilson (1977) found that complete strangers can often make more accurate predictions as to how we might react to something than we can ourselves.

Tyrell suggests the following as a summary towards considering ourselves more objectively and learning to bypass self-justifying thoughts:

- Understanding that we do not have immediate conscious access to all our motivations

- Realising that it is easy to make up reasons that flatter us or fit a preconceived pattern of low or high self-esteem but that don't actually match up with the truth

- Accepting that we might be responding automatically to a new person or situation simply because of a superficial resemblance to a previous person or time

- Refraining from jumping to conclusions about our own actions, motivations and responses

- Watching ourselves as calmly and objectively as possible, focusing on what we *do*, not just on what we tell ourselves and other people

(2013, p. 3)

Developing this skill takes a little practice. Sometimes it is a useful exercise to work on it with a good coach, though not all coaches will understand the idea. A good starting point is to find a place where you will not be disturbed, including by phone calls. Identify a situation that is currently on your agenda. Explore your feelings around the situation, perhaps asking what your inner dialogue was saying at the time. If the issue centres around an individual, what were your judgements, perhaps even prejudices around this person? What did I say? Could I have handled the situation differently? What will my next steps be?

Consider doing this twice a day, perhaps for five to ten minutes. Keeping a journal can be very helpful. There are a number of good articles that can be found online. The University of Worcester (2016) produce a succinct plan for doing this. One caveat: please be careful about confidentiality. Deploying the observational self can be particularly useful when dealing with challenging situations and, indeed, people. You do not, however, want your reflections to become a new version of WikiLeaks. You might consider using code in your reflections so that individuals are not identified, or keep it on your computer using encryption.

As a postscript, I would like to return to the 1961 Milgram experiment. This has been the subject of review, replication and debate for many years. It has been utilised in television programmes and films, *eg* Derren Brown drew on it for his 2006 film *The Heist*. Central to the debate has been the ethical issues involved. The story has often been spun in different ways.

There was a replication of the original experiment carried out at La Trobe University in the early 1970s. Perry explored the outcomes in her book *Behind the Shock Machine* (2012). She noted that a number of participants suffered long-term psychological disturbance after participating in the experiment.

It is reasonable to offer the caveat that if leaders coerce staff, or indeed pupils, to go against their personal moral stance, there is a chance that emotional damage will be done. Certainly, the clients that I have worked with demonstrated significant levels of stress. Many came after making problematic career decisions following their implication with the examination malpractice. A leader surely has a responsibility not to impose ill-founded and excessive direction that could potentially override a colleague's moral parameters and which could lead to a degree of personal disintegration.

8. HEADS AND TALES

Yes, in all my research, the greatest leaders looked inward and were able to tell a good story with authenticity and passion.

(Deepak Chopra)

Several years ago, I had the privilege of working with the storytelling guru, Steve Denning. Denning had developed the idea of using narrative in his leadership role at the World Bank. Immersed in the inevitability of change – that is, the experience of organisational culture which is indeed the experience of us all – he began to realise the importance of narrative as a vehicle that would transform thinking and in turn change practice. Though there needs to be a bedrock of rationality and evidence underpinning change there also needs to be a connection with people to facilitate their embracing change. PowerPoints seldom change beliefs. Denning has argued:

> The physical science has had an aversion to anything to do with storytelling in part because it deals with such murky things as intentions, emotions and matters of the heart. Yet in the past couple of decades, most of the human sciences have grasped the centrality of narrative to human affairs. Narrative has come to be influential in vast regions of psychology, anthropology, philosophy, sociology, political theory, literary studies, religious studies, psychotherapy and even medicine. Management is amongst the last of the disciplines to recognise the central significance of narrative to the issues that it deals with.
>
> (Denning, 2011, p. 11)

Leading and managing change is a core activity for leaders at all levels within organisations. Storytelling is, perhaps, the greatest omission from many leaders' skillsets. However, narrative as a leadership competency, though crucial, is not the focus of this chapter. We rely on our construction of story to make sense of our world. In this we are script-writer, producer, director and usually have the starring role in most of our productions.

As we tell our stories, both to ourselves and to others, the narrative becomes cast as being true. For many people, this is a major misconception, as ultimately, they are simply our stories and become interlaced to form our metanarrative. When the Portuguese explorer Ferdinand Magellan mounted an expedition to circumnavigate the world, it must have been challenging to recruit when the prevailing belief was that the world was discoid, with dragons at the edge. The inviolate belief people have in their stories surfaces within such areas as the delusional support of failing football clubs, the fan base of bands, political opinion and religion, to name but a few.

If a person's story is deconstructed by circumstances then the impact can be considerable. Gail had accumulated considerable personal baggage. As a child, she had been adopted into a family that had never felt like a good fit. She is an able individual but she had drifted away from a demanding job into a rather disparate existence supported by several student lets. A long-term relationship had ended unexpectedly. She became relatively isolated but had links with one supportive family. She progressively associated with the family, extending her influence and dismantling boundaries as to make them her surrogate family. Eventually, her incursions created tensions with the family members who began to reinstate boundaries and in the process challenged the delusional story that Gail had been telling herself that she had moved from being a friend to being a family member. As the family began to erect fences, her behaviour became increasingly vindictive and her narrative more and more confused.

Holding your own

Most people like to think that they are fair and open-minded, ready to be convinced by another person's point of view. This is a commendable aspiration but one which is often at odds with experience. People seem to be able to hold on to viewpoints with incredible tenacity in the face of contradictory information, and leaders are no different. Many of us have known for a long time that other people do this. It is salutary to reflect on our own personal aptitude for bias.

Consider two people arguing as to whether they would rather drive a Volvo or a Ford. Certainly, technical information might come into the discussion: brake horsepower, customer satisfaction surveys, fuel economy and acceleration *etc.* The reality is that they are both good cars and yet a comment such as 'I wouldn't be seen dead in (insert the vehicle of choice here)' is not an impressive indicator of cognitive processing. The science fiction writer Heinlein nailed it when he observed 'Man is not a rational animal, he is a rationalizing animal' (1953, p. 27).

This ability of human beings to defend their subjective narrative or belief set has been explored by psychologists such as Lord, Ross and Lepper (1979). They presented subjects with evidence supporting or rejecting the effectiveness of capital punishment to a group of subjects who held divergent views on this subject. They selected 24 capital punishment protagonists and the same number of antagonists. After reading a given article on capital punishment, the participants were then shown critiques of the article. These included procedure, results, prominent criticisms and results shown in a table or graph. They were then asked to evaluate the study as to its rigour and how convincing was their view of the evidence.

At the end of the experiment there was an even greater polarisation of views amongst some participants than the researchers had expected. The participants found that studies that supported their pre-existing view were superior to those that contradicted it. In fact, the studies all described the same experimental procedure with only the purported result being changed. This propensity to select evidence and viewpoints which are in line with our own has been termed 'confirmation bias'.

Even more intriguing was the study undertaken by Westen *et al* (2006). A sample of committed Democrats and Republicans were the focus of a study during the three months prior to the US Presidential Elections of 2004. Each group was given the task of considering threatening or contradictory information relating to their candidate of choice: John Kerry or George Bush respectively. Functional neuroimaging (fMRI) was used to study how they were processing the information in their brains.

The fMRI showed that the emotional areas of their brains activated but they but did not see any increased activation of the parts of the brain normally associated with reasoning. It was a network of emotion-based areas that lit up in the scan. This included parts of the brain that have been hypothesised as being involved in regulating emotion, and also areas linked to resolving conflicts.

After reading the material, the participants all returned to their original viewpoint and found ways to discard contradictory information in order to sustain their established position. Of course, the discrediting information related to the opposing candidate was gratefully received. Once their preferred bias had been restored the brain rewarded itself with a secretion of dopamine. This would produce a pleasant high and would tend to confirm the 'rightness' of moving back to their original and preferred position.

The inclusion of research into confirmation bias is not about engendering self-doubt or undermining self-confidence. It is about arguing that those in leadership roles should ensure that systems are in place to check their own views, policies, vision and perceptions. This is a part of the strength of effective teams and it again justifies the regular interface with a competent coach. The latter can explore and challenge the story that you inhabit. As Shakespeare adroitly observed: 'There is nothing either good or bad, but thinking makes it so'.

Through the looking glass

> I know who I WAS when I got up this morning, but I think I must have been changed several times since then.
>
> (Alice, *Alice's Adventures in Wonderland*
> Carroll, 2014)

I have suggested that many of us defend our particular versions of events because it has a link to our identity and the mechanism by which this is done. Confirmation bias has also been outlined. In general terms, this is true, and we usually defend 'our truth' even in the face of contradictory facts and information. Our narrative can also become unstable and this can be fuelled by stress. This is particularly the case in the focus that we give to particular aspects of our story and also in terms of the way that we aggregate individual sub plots to generate a changed narrative. Our internal as well as our external narrative can move from positive to negative extremely quickly.

One fascinating example of how our chain linking of fragments of our story can change our whole perspective and also our emotional state is a process called catastrophisation. The best illustration of this comes from a homely domestic interchange between my wife, Sally, and myself. However, once you are aware of it you will notice that this is commonplace in conversations. Our eldest son, then in his mid-twenties, had been made redundant. He had been applying for jobs and on this particular day had a promising interview with a local firm. I had been in London and arrived back home around 10.30*pm*. The dialogue went like this:

(Me) 'How did David get on? Did he get the job?'

(Sally) 'No, it was a real shame, he didn't get the job. Of course, these are difficult times with the economy. Nobody's got jobs. David will never get a job. He'll never leave home and you won't be able to retire and you'll die.'

This was spectacular especially as the whole conversation took less than 40 seconds. This was catastrophising at its best (or worst?).

Humans have, as far as we can tell, a unique ability to ruminate about the past and project possible scenarios into the future. Even though these may not be real – and certainly they will not be current – they have the capacity to reset the emotions, especially if they are negative. A brief consideration of PTSD will provide a powerful example of how time-distanced events can drive the now. So catastrophisation needs to be eliminated. If you find yourself going down this line, pause and then commit to coming up with at least three alternative scenarios that you could use to describe the situation.

Such ambiguity can be of great benefit in dialling down inappropriate certainties that we may have and hold. The more that we can say 'maybe', the greater will be the range of resources that are likely to be available to us; this is in contrast with concrete certainty, which narrows our focus and will marshal a particular set of resources to effect a specific course of action. This runs counter to the narrowing impact of stress, which tries to move us towards 'all-or-nothing thinking'.

This Chinese fable makes this point and also demonstrates how stories can engage with us emotionally as well:

Once there was a farmer who had a handsome and strong horse. The horse was not only beautiful to look at but helped supply the income on which the man and his family depended.

But one night, the horse escaped and ran off. All the other villagers were deeply sympathetic towards the farmer and his loss. They came to offer their condolences at such a massive loss.

'What a terrible thing to have happened,' they said to the man. But he just shrugged and calmly said, 'Maybe...or maybe not.' They were surprised at his attitude, sangfroid and nonchalant, and soon went about their day.

A few days later, the farmer's beautiful stallion returned with 12 beautiful mares in tow. This was a real bonus.

All the locals were quick to congratulate him. 'What wonderful luck for you!' they cried. But again, the man, chilled to the core, said: 'Well... maybe...or maybe not. Let's wait and see, shall we?' Once more, the villagers were nonplussed by his attitude but felt pleased for him anyway.

The very next day, the man's son was taming one of the wild horses when he fell and broke his leg. 'What bad luck!' cried the villagers. 'Maybe it's good luck; maybe it's bad luck. We'll have to wait and see.' said the man.

'Really?' said the villagers, who were getting tired of his apparent fatalism. 'Please tell us, how on earth can your son breaking his leg not be considered to be bad luck!?' And they went about their business.

But just a few days later, royal messengers came to the village proclaiming that all young men were to be immediately drafted into the army for the purpose of serving in an unjust and, as it turned out, hopeless and destructive war. But the man's son, having just broken his leg, was rejected for service. The entire company he would have enlisted with soon perished in one of the very first assaults of the war.

All the other villagers came to the old man and now said, 'Whew, what good luck that your son was spared fighting and being killed in the war!' The man just smiled, but they knew what he was thinking.

(Author Unknown)

The farmer in the fable is depicted as someone who does not assume – or, more importantly, does not catastrophise – but waits to see the emerging truth of the situation. Uncertainty is not the same as ambiguity. The former is about indecision, the latter is about not rushing to fill the meaning vacuum. I would suggest, as an aside, that if we have children, 'ambiguity' is one of the greatest gifts that we can give them.

Everything changes

When we are (dis)stressed, everything changes: the focus of our attention narrows, we become preoccupied with ourselves to the exclusion of others, our language changes, we move towards what is often described as 'all-or-nothing thinking'. We have moved into survival mode, which is definitely the wrong vantage point from which to lead an organisation.

Imagine that you experiencing overlapping challenges. Perhaps these could be coming from a variety of your personal and professional circumstances. Such incidents are also quite likely to have some people-related problems in the mix as well. Theoretically, we handle such challenges with professionalism and objectivity. Realistically, there will be days or even quite prolonged periods when situations and problems get under our guard and stress-related physiology is triggered.

When we become (dis)stressed, our vocabulary changes. Negative hyperbole begins to move to the fore: terrible, disaster, impossible, the list goes on. Problems are red lights on the dashboard. Using the word 'issue' has a completely different feel: it sponsors problem-solving rather than initiating problem-driven panic.

Underpinning the words, (dis)stress rapidly causes us to explain things differently. Pause for a moment and consider the phrases in the left column and suggest which are associated with a calm state and which are likely to occur when someone is stressed.

Explanation	The meaning 'spin' given to it
Internal or External *Me or not me*	**Internal:** 'It's my fault or responsibility' **External:** 'It's someone else's fault, that's a pity'
Global or Specific *Everything or 'Just this'*	**Global:** 'My whole life is ruined' **Specific:** 'That's spoilt that bit of what I was doing'
Stable or Unstable *Forever or temporary*	**Stable:** 'This will last for ever' **Unstable:** 'Things will change over time'

Table 8.0 Explanatory or attributional styles (Adapted from Elliott and Tyrell, 2002, p. 37)

The stressed person will see the situation as being their fault (Internal), the problem will impact them as a whole (Global) and bad things will have a persistence or permanency (Stable). This change in our language will neither inspire nor motivate others and it will reduce our own performance as we focus internally and begin to lose connection with our wider context.

The snowball

Stories serve a purpose by making sense of our world. Negative stories also serve a purpose by giving expression to a perceived threat or by identifying circumstances that our limbic centre feels we should retreat from. Of course, in a difficult professional situation, we will stay; after all, we are leaders and sorting things out is what we do: perhaps our sense of vocation will not let us walk away, and then there are our financial needs that have to be met by our salary. So, our fight-or-flight mechanism has cut in – not to be awkward, but to try and protect us from a perceived threat – but is being overruled by our rational brain.

There is now a stand-off, but the limbic centre ups its game and starts to intensify the negative story by collecting and reinterpreting more information as negative. This is not perverse, this is just how we are set up. Pleasant memories are largely taken for granted, it is the negative ones that are used as a mechanism to provoke protective action. This negative enhancement is rather like a snowball rolling down a hill and getting bigger as it rolls. I once used this illustration in Saudi Arabia; with hindsight, a snow-based simile was not a good idea, though it did create a fascinating conversation.

This tension between the cognitive intractability and limbic centre's escalating negalogue can go on for quite some time. Circumstances can change and the threat can subside or the intensity can increase and potentially become a driver of depression.

9. NIGHTSHIFT

The machinery is always going. Even when you are asleep.

(Andy Warhol)

It had been one of those days; the intentions of the morning had given way to the frustrations of the afternoon. The unexpected had progressively eclipsed the 'to-do list'. Arriving home at 7.30*pm*, you ate a meal with no recollection of what you had eaten. Two hours were spent catching up with unfinished work from the day. Finally, exhausted, you managed to get into bed, sliding between freshly laundered sheets, echoing Quasimodo's cry of 'Sanctuary'. Nothing could be further from the truth. This is where a session of serious work is about to begin. If sleep does not progress in a defined pattern, there will be serious consequences in terms of wellbeing and personal efficacy. Disturbed sleep is not simply about feeling tired at the start of the following day it is about leaving life events in untidy stacks in our heads and leaving emotional loops unresolved.

The inner game of sleep

Most of us spend approximately one third of our lives sleeping, or at least trying to sleep. A simple survey will soon show that many people have little idea of what is happening beyond a having a somewhat vague belief that a good night's sleep is desirable. Robotham *et al* make the argument for sleep as a core human activity:

> Sleep affects our ability to use language, sustain attention, understand what we are reading and summarise what we are hearing. If we compromise on our sleep, we compromise on our performance, our mood and our interpersonal relationships.

> (2011, p. 13)

Good sleep is held to have a series of five stages, and in turn these groupings occur some four or five times each night, with each cycle taking around 90 minutes. The first stage is light sleep, almost an interface between being awake and being asleep. This is the stage where we can get those strange twitches called hypnic jerks. A few minutes later we move into Stage 2, not dissimilar to Stage 1 but that bit deeper with muscles relaxing, eye movement stopping and a slowing of heart and breathing rates. This stage accounts for nearly 50% of human sleep but it is still fairly shallow and someone woken at this point could well deny that they have even been asleep.

Stages 3 and 4 are normally grouped together and the distinction between them is technical and is linked to the proportion of different brain waves. This stage is often referred to as slow-wave sleep. This type of sleep is refreshing, and waking someone from this stage will often result in the sleeper feeling disorientated and they will appear only semi coherent. Importantly, this is where what has been learnt during the day is processed and incorporated into our memories. It is in some ways like saving a document or spreadsheet to the hard drive.

The final stage of each cycle, if all is going to plan, is rapid eye movement (REM) sleep. This takes its name from the discernible eye movements that can be seen under the closed eyelids. The breathing rate rises, as does the heart rate. Concurrently, the major muscle groups become paralysed so that we cannot move our arms and legs.

It is during REM sleep that we begin to dream. Mystery still surrounds the role of dreaming. Some contend that important emotional processing is taking place, whilst others seem to suggest that they are little more than a device to keep the brain occupied so that the sleeper does not wake up (Solms, 2000). In the following chapter, the argument is made that, whilst there is still a great deal to be discovered about REM sleep, its role is considerably more important than being a psychological Netflix.

These five stages, which are iterative, are regulated by a mechanism called a circadian timer working in tandem with the sleep homeostat. The latter is a regulator that secures adequate amounts of sleep and can implement a payback process if we have built up a sleep debt through not being able to get sufficient sleep over the preceding period. This complex feedback mechanism is controlled by periods of light and darkness. The way these two interact is shown below:

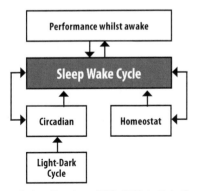

Figure 9.0 Sleep homeostat and circadian timer (Dijk, 2010, in Robotham *et al*, 2011, p. 17)

Too much detail? However, it does give an indication that this watch-like mechanism is susceptible to being thrown out of kilter.

> A prolonged period of stress or worry can also affect our ability to sleep. In a sample of roughly 20,000 young adults, lack of sufficient sleep was linked to psychological distress.
>
> Robotham *et al* (2011, p. 31)

Sleep walking

Sleepio is an organisation exploring sleep patterns and also providing advice to help people improve the quality of their sleep. They also conduct regular surveys of sleeping habits in the UK. The data used below is taken from their 2011 and 2012 surveys. Their findings provide insights as to how sleep empowers performance and its lack will cause us to operate below par.

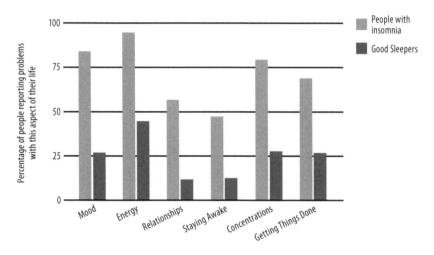

Graph 9.0 The Negative impact of poor sleep on daily life (Robotham *et al*, 2011, p. 31)

The data from the survey, presented here as a graph, is unequivocal in showing that the effects of poor sleep have a major impact on our daily activities. When a comparison is made between good sleepers and their sleep deprived counterparts, many in the latter group have reported having four times as many relationship difficulties. The results also show that low mood increases with poor sleep patterns, as does an increased susceptibility to depression.

Insomniac respondents reported issues around reduced concentration and poor energy levels. They found difficulty in 'getting things done' and staying awake.

The latter would certainly affect performance at work. However, in turn a failure to cope with tasks effectively will inevitably increase anxiety and (dis)stress.

The survey of the following year (2012) displayed similar trends. Poor sleepers in comparison with those with good sleep patterns are:

- seven times more likely to feel helpless.

- five times more likely to feel alone.

- three times more likely to struggle to concentrate.

- twice as likely to suffer from fatigue.

- twice as likely to have relationship problems.

- twice as likely to suffer low mood.

- twice as likely to be unproductive.

(Sleepio, 2012, p. 3)

The extension of these findings to include feelings around helplessness and a perception of being isolated should be of concern to all of us, but the impact of the context of leadership will become a significant threat to wellbeing.

Dreams are made of this

Securing a good night's sleep should be high on all of our personal agendas. The challenging question is: how much sleep do we need? There is no definitive answer to this question. A new-born baby may sleep for 18 hours a day whilst someone in middle age may manage with as little as five hours each night. The structure of sleep may vary with young people who record a greater incidence of REM sleep. This is probably linked to brain maturation. REM sleep is also associated with the plasticity of neuronal networks, which could help with the acquisition of new skills.

Taking a slight detour, Dijk and Winsky-Sommerer (2012) noted that during adolescence sleep becomes shallower and shifts to later hours. They also argued that:

> The frontal lobe – responsible for executive functions such as planning and inhibiting inappropriate behaviour – shows a marked fall in synapse density as the result of neuronal pruning. Teenagers are not just being lazy when they don't want to get out of bed. Their adolescent biology may also prefer an adjustment of school hours.

> There is good evidence that young people don't get enough sleep. When they live on an 8-hour sleep schedule they remain sleepy, and much more

so than older people on the same schedule. If young adults are forced to stay in bed in darkness for 16 hours a day they initially sleep for as long as 12 hours. However, after several days they level off to just under 9 hours, showing that they were paying off a sleep debt.

(2012, p. 3)

Whilst it is difficult to be precise about the amount of sleep that we need, it is indisputable that we all need good quality sleep if we are to remain well and to function at a high level. There are many reasons why people suffer from insomnia and it is advisable to seek medical advice if you are not sleeping on a regular basis. What follows is general advice that will help you sleep well:

1. **Relax before going to bed.** Take time for a pre-sleep ritual to break the link between your daytime activity and bedtime. You might try some mindfulness, reading or a shower.

2. **Avoid caffeine.** Coffee, tea, and hot chocolate generally contain the stimulant caffeine.

3. **Note anything on your mind.** If there is something that you are thinking about, or something that you need to remember, write it down in a notebook. The latter is better than scraps of paper, which can be lost, and better than a smartphone, which should not be in the bedroom anyway!

4. **Limit alcohol consumption.** Alcoholic drinks may help you to fall asleep, but as your body clears the alcohol from your system, you are likely to wake up. It can also cause disturbing dreams, sweating and headaches. Drinking one glass of water for every unit of alcohol consumed will help but then you begin to run into problems associated with number 6!

5. **Your bed is for sleeping in.** Your mind attaches significance to particular locations. It is helpful to build an expectation that this is the place where sleep happens. It is useful to avoid TV, digital devices, intense discussions and even eating when you are in bed.

6. **No drinks after 8.00***pm***.** This can seem harsh but if you wish to avoid trips to the 'loo' during the night then this is sound advice unless there are medical reasons why you should continue with your fluid intake.

7. **Eat for sleep.** Avoid eating a large meal just before bedtime and conversely do not go to bed hungry. Sleep-supportive snacks include:

milk, tuna, almonds, eggs, peaches, oats, asparagus, potatoes and
bananas.

8. **Exercise at the right time.** Regular exercise can relieve stress and
    encourage sleep. However, exercising in the latter part of the evening
    to the extent that your blood is pumping will probably stimulate you
    too much.

9. **Create the right environment.** Your bedroom should be a quiet
    pace with subdued lighting and a temperature around 20-22 degrees
    Celsius. If you read, it is better to have a point source of light rather
    than raising the overall level of lighting in the room.

10. **Power nap.** There are many advocates of the daytime power nap and
    in some countries some level of sleep during the day is part of the
    culture. However, if you routinely fall asleep in the evening then the
    support act will eclipse the star attraction.

This chapter, 'Nightshift', has explored the importance of sleep in terms of
our performance. The following chapter, 'Living the Dream', links to this idea
and takes our understanding further with a particular focus on securing our
wellbeing and avoiding depression. Chapter 14, 'Digifree', also has advice on
the impact of digital devices and considers their adverse effect on our sleep.
Sometimes, we are own worst enemies by not making adequate preparations for
this vital part of our lives. After all, if we spend one-third of our lives sleeping or
attempting to sleep, let us at least take such a vital process seriously.

10. LIVING THE DREAM

How will we better contain depression? Expect no magic pill. One lesson learned from treating chronic pain is that it is tough to override responses that are hardwired into the body and the mind. Instead, we must follow the economy of mood where it leads, attending to the sources that brings so many into low mood states-think routines that feature too much work and too little sleep. We need broader mood literacy and an awareness of tools that interact low mood states before they morph into longer more severe ones. These tools include altering how we think the events around us, our relationships, and conditions in our body.

(Rottenberg, 2014, p. 32)

In the 1950s, my father worked as a technical representative for Stafford-based grinding wheel company. He used to visit a factory in Leeds that made asbestos-based building products such as roofing materials and downpipes. Several streets from the factory, children would have 'snowball fights' with toxic asbestos waste. The actual conditions in the factory must have been terminal. There are many occupational-based diseases, such as pneumoconiosis for miners, or even mercury poisoning experienced by Victorian hatters, an occupation immortalised by Lewis Carroll. Anxiety and depression are also widespread in the workplace. Even so, school leaders, and indeed teachers themselves, would be justified in making a claim for these as their occupation-related disease.

Flintham (2003b) conducted research amongst headteachers in Nottingham. In essence, he conducted exit interviews with school leaders who had resigned their posts. Some had retired, some moved to other schools, but he also found a cohort that had retired prematurely. Some of the accounts in his research are distressing. One secondary headteacher that he interviewed recorded:

> I was very good at hiding it. Other heads and my staff didn't know the extent of my angst until I lost it through a panic attack at a heads' meeting. I went long-term sick and had to retire early on health grounds. I've cut myself off from education. I've never been back to my school and at first I couldn't even face the people I'd worked with if I met them elsewhere. I don't work at all now.
>
> (2003b, p. 8)

Sadly, such unaddressed issues continue to take a heavy toll within the profession. In its survey in 2016, the NASUWT found that:

- 5% said they had increased their use of tobacco.

- 14% had undergone counselling.

- 5% have been admitted to hospital.

- over three-quarters (79%) had reported experiencing work-related anxiousness.

- 86% had suffered sleeplessness and a third reported poor health.

- 2% of teachers said they had self-harmed as a result of work-related pressures.

These figures stand in a wider context of a depression epidemic. It has been estimated that people born since 1945 are ten times more likely to suffer from depression than those born before this date (Seligman, 1988). This is startling, particularly when you consider that many of those born before 1945 went through the World Wars and suffered associated deprivation.

What it is and what it does

Robert had been the principal of a secondary academy for five years. His contribution to its development was seen as being significant and positive. Unexpectedly, a series of issues cascaded to generate high levels of personal stress. He had challenged the unacceptable performance of the head of the maths department, and it had rapidly escalated into an unpleasant stand-off as she was signed off with stress. Sadly, the lady had also suffered a miscarriage and her union representative accused Robert of causing this as a result of initiating formal proceedings. Compassionate by nature, this affected Robert deeply. National changes to the funding formula had created a budget shortfall and he was wrestling with a solution where the headline strategy appeared to be to make a number of staff redundant. A recent IT system had taken malfunction to the level beyond 'teething problems' and there was now a legal dispute taking place with the supplier. He also had a further staff performance issue in his in-tray, which was creating problems as the member of staff was also absent and he could not fill the void left in a specialist subject. At a personal level, Robert was also facing anxiety. His father, who had suffered from Parkinson's Disease, was becoming increasingly infirm and unable to maintain independent living. When he snatched less-pressured moments, he felt guilty about his detachment from his wife and his teenage children. Dark clouds had suddenly appeared in what had been a clear blue sky.

He was aware that he was being affected by these events: he was exhausted; simple tasks were beginning to feel insurmountable; he suffered from mood swings; as his confidence ebbed away, hope seemed a distant horizon and increasingly anger and criticism were becoming personal motifs. Normally socially gregarious, he was now starting to detach himself from people and realised that he was becoming increasingly self-absorbed and ruminating on his problems. Whilst he was not particularly keen on hobbies, he did enjoy walking his dog and eating out. A moment's reflection revealed a somewhat neglected dog and a growing number of unmemorable meals.

Feeling less than his best, Robert had sought medical advice. His GP assured him that there was no underlying pathology such as heart disease or thyroid problems. He diagnosed Robert as being depressed and suggested that he took time off work for at least a month and also that he should start a course of anti-depressants. These were not his solutions of choice. Being absent for a month seemed to be the stuff of fantasy. He decided not to take the anti-depressants after an internet search about their potential side effects. There seemed to be some evidence that they could impair his core role as a decision-maker (Crockett *et al*, 2015).

Seamlessly, anxiety had morphed into depression.

The structure of depression

Robert had become overwhelmed by challenging circumstances but context was not the total explanation for his plight. All of us find that many of the problems and issues that we have to deal with have an attached emotional tag. Taking action against the head of maths was not just a simple HR issue: institute a process and appoint a replacement, job done. For many leaders, experiences like this create anxiety and rumination. In this example, the situation was exacerbated by the allegations made by an aggressive union representative. Such emotional tags will usually trigger a stress state and in turn this will change our style of thinking. The brain will also try to bring such emotional arousal to completion, if this is not achieved during the day then it will end up in the inbox of REM sleep.

Depressed people will use language which reflects their retreat into a tight inner focus and place themselves very much in the centre. Their statements will become increasingly black and white or what is often typified as 'all-or-nothing thinking'. A depressed person will tend to talk in terms of the situation 'as always being like this' or a potential resolution as being 'the only alternative'. The latter somehow feels like an oxymoron but people still use the expression. They will often perceive good things as temporary and random whilst bad things are understood as being permanent and deserved. If you remember the discussion of the fight-or-flight response introduced in Chapter 1, it was argued that stress inhibits alternatives in order to facilitate a rapid response to an immediate and non-deferrable threat. This begins to explain many of the hallmarks of depression: the blindness to consider the needs of others, the failure to engage with amorphous tasks, the disregard of the longer term and the impact of the adrenaline rush and the activation of the amygdala that leads to anger.

The second issue is the need to try to bring any extant emotional arousal to completion. Consider again the problem facing Robert with the potential budget deficit. This issue, also, has a strong emotional tag. He has no alternative but to balance the books, and because of the way school budgets are structured, a deficit usually means reducing staff. In this case, in order to preserve the curriculum provision, his most likely solution is to reduce the number of teaching assistants (TAs). A number of these TAs have been brought on within the school and had been encouraged to consider becoming Higher Level Teaching Assistants (HLTAs). One person potentially in the frame for redundancy had already begun to consider becoming a teacher. The thought of dashing these peoples' hopes and ambitions was extremely painful to him.

So, Robert finds himself faced with a number of pressing problems to which there are no easy answers. These are not like dealing with an irate parent or taking an assembly or chairing a staff briefing. Rittell and Webber (1973) formalised the description of these kind of problems as being 'wicked'. These are problems which often lack clear definition and where the solution is pragmatic rather than absolute. However, what is clear is that, for the leader, these kinds of problems become portable and soon become constant companions.

These problems with their attached unclosed emotional loops take us back to the chapter title, 'Living the Dream'. These unresolved loops are the substance of dreams as the brain creates scenarios and metaphorically acts these out in an attempt to close the loop. For example, anxiety caused by someone making critical comments about you could manifest in a dream where you are mugged and beaten up. Dreams occur during the REM phases of our sleep; this process is our emotional launderette. The previous chapter, 'Nightshift', has already described sleep as being not only busy but also important. Dreaming is hard work.

If our dreaming does not manage to close these emotional loops then we will sow the seeds of depression in the tilth of pessimistic and narrowed patterns of language. Attempts to resolve these demand that more and more time is spent in REM sleep, and this also begins to appear earlier in the sleep cycle. A depressed person does up to three times as much dreaming in the REM state that a non-depressed person does. Further, in a person who is not depressed, REM sleep cuts in some 90 minutes after falling asleep, whereas in a depressed person it can start as quickly as three minutes after falling asleep. When we engage in REM sleep, serotonin is depleted. Serotonin (there are actually quite a few types) serves a number of functions, including sponsoring our physical motivation. However, during REM sleep it helps suppress muscle movement; we become almost paralysed to ensure that our dreams remain metaphorical and are not acted out in a potentially dangerous manner. With this depletion of serotonin, we wake enervated and find we really are not set up to get going physically. Serotonin is a neurotransmitter with a role which also includes generating feelings of fulfilment or completion. Imagine pushing your chair back after a satisfying meal feeling replete; that is very much the sort of feeling it generates. If, however, it has been depleted from an excess of REM sleep, we are also more likely to feel empty, aimless and purposeless. A lack of serotonin does not cause depression, but rather depression leads to its depletion. Slow-wave sleep is minimised and so refreshment and healing can be inhibited as well. A significant part of the package of depression is over-dreaming.

Reset

Depression should never be trivialised, either in ourselves or in others. The fact that it is the most prevalent mental health issue makes it no less serious and it can easily become the gateway to incapacity and even self-harm. If you suspect you are depressed or that a colleague or friend is treading this well-worn path then medical advice should be sought or strongly advocated. If, as you are reading this, you are already taking prescription medication for anxiety or depression, please do not stop taking it or alter the dosage without discussing matters with your doctor. Advice or strategy in this chapter – or indeed, in the book as a whole – can be used in tandem with medical intervention.

The above is very much a 'flypast' of the subject of depression. This evidence-based perspective of both explanatory style and the role of over-dreaming has been of benefit to many people in moving on from the debilitating effects of depression. A much more extensive and indeed practical consideration is given in *How to lift depression...fast* (Griffin and Tyrell, 2014a).

The following strategies will certainly be effective in pulling us out of the quagmire of depression and they are also useful to prevent us bogging down in the first place.

1. Understand how depression works. If we can see how it operates, we can intercept the behaviours that are driving the cycle. Once we are clear how depression works and that our situation can be changed, a

light will begin to appear at the end of the tunnel: hope. Development of these insights is best done routinely outside a depressive episode so that you have tools which are both preventative and curative at your disposal – but it is never too late to use them.

2. As a leader, audit your life on a weekly basis and really commit to this with no downtime. Flintham (2003b) in his research noted how frequently the metaphor was used of the frog that fails to jump from a pan of water that is being slowly heated until it boils to death. An audit process is detailed in Chapter 20.

3. Secure good sleeping patterns so that the toll of over-dreaming is avoided or minimised. This will significantly reduce the fatigue and the joint and muscle pains that are so often the hallmarks of depression.

4. It is useful to 'listen in' to our conversations, both internal and external. Are our stories becoming pessimistic? Is our language increasingly peppered with 'all-or-nothing phrases' that give away our restricted and damaging thinking? Does our self-talk condemn us? It would be useful to notice whether we speak to others in an uninterested, angry or irritated fashion. Are we taken up with too much meaning-making and catastrophisation? We can check on ourselves by using the observational self technique (Chapter 8) or explore our language and phraseology and how to reframe our narrative with a good coach (Chapter 18).

5. One of the single most successful strategies for resetting depression is mindfulness (Chapter 19). It has been estimated that we exist 'in the moment' for a mere two hours during the time that we are formally awake. The remainder of the time, we try to understand past events or we move into an inappropriate prophetic mode as we try to anticipate the future. Mindfulness brings us back to the present and reduces rumination. It is like pulling up in a layby with an overheated engine and changing into neutral and letting the engine idle. Routinely practising mindfulness has an enduring effect by helping us view problems in a less intense and pressing manner. When I work with depressed or anxious clients, this (now widely known) technique is welcomed as being a positive strategy. In many cases, however, the benefits are negated if the client is not practising it on a daily basis. A two-day trial will change little. I suspect that this is also why, as many schools have introduced staff and pupils to the technique, the results

have often been indifferent and even greeted with cynicism. That is the equivalent of the diabetic leaving their insulin in the medicine cabinet. Perhaps singing 'Let It Go' from Disney's *Frozen* (2013) should be mandatory for leaders. (This should probably only be done in tightly prescribed situations to avoid damaging personal credibility.)

6. Ensure that you make time for pleasure, fun or social activity. It is important that this is something that appeals to you and is not an activity which someone else feels that you should do. Sometimes this might require making an effort and moving out of your temporary, depressed, discomfort zone.

7. When we are depressed, we become self-absorbed and almost anything that expands our interpersonal horizons will be beneficial. The positive psychologist Martin Seligman (2008) suggests setting up a 'gratitude visit'. You are asked to think of someone who has made a significant positive contribution to your life but is unaware of the fact. Seligman suggests writing down a 300-word testimonial and then making an appointment to go and see them but not to declare the intended purpose of your visit. Seligman admits that the meeting will be emotional but in a good way. This is an interesting technique but probably it would not be appropriate for someone who was feeling at a particularly low point.

8. Healthy diet and exercise – these will always help our general health. Exercise been recognised as being particularly beneficial (Craft and Perna, 2004).

9. If you have not exercised for a long time or are concerned about the effects of exercise on your body or health, ask your GP about exercise on prescription. Many GP surgeries across the country prescribe exercise as a treatment for a range of conditions, including depression.

10. Spend time with people who are not depressed. They do not need to be stand-up comedians but some level of positivity will certainly be beneficial. Some 15 years ago I experienced a significant bout of depression. I was off work and I was invited round for coffee by a friend in similar circumstances. In the three weeks that he had been off work, he had become a leading expert on depression. What he did not know about possible medication and counselling really was not worth knowing. I left determined to avoid him and find some more uplifting company. Now, all these years on, he is still being treated

for depression, and sadly he has developed 'depression as lifestyle'. I will come clean, I went and spent a week with a friend, camping and making a chair using a pole lathe. The friend was just this side of *Live at the Apollo*. You cannot get an experience like this on the NHS, but it did reinforce the fact that the opposite of depression is not happiness but peace!

11. Counselling, one of the talking therapies. This can be useful but a depressed person should avoid psychodynamic counsellors who seek to explore the past. If you are depressed then a future-focused therapy, rather than one which supports rumination about the past, will win the day. Interestingly, in America some psychodynamic counsellors have been sued by clients who have come to them with depression and found themselves to be in a worse state than when they started their therapy (Elliott and Griffin, 2002).

Afterword

Life events, including those from our professional life, can be seen to trigger depression. Depression is not, however, caused by what happens to us, it is about how we respond and make sense of these events. This understanding of how depression is constructed has been developed by Griffin and Tyrell:

> The important thing is to know how depression is manufactured in the brain. Once you understand that, you can correct the maladaptive cycle incredibly fast. For 40 years it's been known that depressed people have excessive REM sleep. They dream far more than healthy people. What we realised – and proved – is that the negative introspection, or ruminations, that depressed people engage in actually causes the excessive dreaming. So, depression is being generated on a 24-hour cycle and we can make a difference within 24 hours to how a person feels.
>
> (2014b, p. 6)

11. THE MYTHOLOGY OF RESILIENCE

I still enjoy playing some of those early Straits songs, and I'm proud of what we did, and certainly we had some great times. It's what we all wanted when we were kids. But you've got to have the resilience to ride that thing, to pick up that ball and run with it. Because you will keep picking it up and keep running.

(Mark Knopfler)

As a child (OK, I will come clean, I was an adult) I liked watching the Roadrunner cartoons. They usually featured dire reprisals by Roadrunner, a fast-running flightless bird, against the predator, Wile E Coyote. At the more sadistic end of the spectrum, the latter was driven into the ground with a hammer, rather like a fence post.

There is currently a great deal of interest in resilience and indeed in running courses to build it with both staff and pupils. However, much of the challenge to peoples' resilience is generated by the activity and leadership of the organisations themselves. The organisation frequently appears to drive individuals into the ground, like Roadrunner pounding Coyote. Frequently, the provided resilience 'training' can become similar to merely providing Coyote with a steel helmet so that the percussion can carry on for longer. The outcome of a lot of this training appears to be an attempt to keep people going for longer, whilst not committing to re-engineering the organisation that is imposing unrealistic problems on staff in the first place. It would seem that training and curriculum initiatives focused on resilience are seeking to defer the toxic consequences of an overheated workplace.

Defining resilience

Literature and films are often based around an individual's struggle against the odds. The 2015 film, *The Revenant*, is very much of that genre. It is about the resilience and fortitude of the hero, Glass, who faces a Native American attack, shelters from the elements in an eviscerated horse carcass, endures self-surgery and near-suffocation. There is also resonance between such resilience and the more archaic term 'moral fibre'. The latter came into common use in the Royal Air Force (RAF) towards the beginning of World War ll. In 1940, RAF commanders were concerned about the high levels of stress amongst their overstretched aircrew. They were instructed to identify men who had lost their confidence and then to distinguish medical cases from those deemed to be 'lacking moral fibre' (Wells, 2014). Subsequently, these men had their files stamped with a large red 'W'. This stood for 'waverer', and it was done to prevent the systemic problem of psychological stress leaking out into the public domain!

It is suggested that a useful working definition of resilience might be: 'the capacity to resist being stalled by adversity'. The following is a more elaborated definition, which can serve as a platform for developing personal resilience:

1. Resilience is the ability to modulate and constructively harness the stress response – a capacity essential to both physical and mental health.

2. Success can hinge on resilience. Setbacks are part of any endeavour and those who act productively will make the most progress.

3. A person can boost his or her resilience. Strategies include reinterpreting negative events, enhancing positive emotions, becoming physically fit, accepting challenges, maintaining a close social network and imitating resilient role models.

(Southwick and Charney, 2013, p. 34)

Four cornerstones of resilience

When it comes to resilience, we are unlikely to start from a common position. Some of us will have a proven track record of being resilient whilst others amongst us are, perhaps, more vulnerable to being derailed when negative events collude against us. There is no absolute 'index of resilience' and how we respond to adversity can also vary with our personal circumstances, our health, tiredness and age. There is no gold standard but all of us can change the odds in favour of increasing our personal resilience. Again, returning to the core theme of this book of stress reduction across extended periods of time, this also holds true for resilience. However, focusing more specifically on resilience, there are four areas which would benefit from our reflection and development:

Reframing: This connects with Chapter 8 – 'Heads and Tales'. The point has been made that we make sense of our experience by casting or framing it as a story. If we allow this, subtly or even precipitously, to move to a negative or even catastrophic narrative then our ability to position ourselves constructively within that situation will be impeded.

Oschner *et al* (2004) found that the reappraisal of an adverse event so that it is seen in less negative terms tends to attenuate a person's positive physiological and psychological reactions to that event. Consider attending a job interview and failing to secure the much-hoped-for post. The common reaction is to defend ourselves by constructing a negative account of what happened, and perhaps becoming hostile to the selection process and to those involved in it. However, taking time to re-evaluate and change the narrative to a more constructive account will reduce our stress. None of us likes to feel rejected and we will rapidly build a story around situations which generate such feelings: 'They didn't give me the chance to explain my strengths'; 'It was a foregone conclusion, they already had somebody else lined up'; 'If only I hadn't stumbled when I answered that one question'; and perhaps most damaging of all, 'Of course, I am not good enough to gain this type of job'.

What would a reframe look like? You could look at the interview as a learning process. It might be helpful to consider if there were any areas of your skills or experience that the interview has highlighted and which would benefit from development. Reflect on any interactions that you had with other candidates – were there tips or ideas that you could use? Suddenly your defensive posture goes, a positive frame is established, and you will feel your energy and resolve returning. These are key components of resilience; you will begin to recharge.

This has been called reframing, or sometimes it is badged as cognitive reappraisal. It leads to an increase in wellbeing and steers you away from bitterness and cynicism, both of which are emotional vampires. Feder *et al* (2008) interviewed 30 former Vietnam prisoners of war about how they now viewed their wartime experiences. Many had reframed their imprisonment, which, for some, had included ill treatment and torture. These ex-prisoners of war had found ways of understanding it such that they had become wiser, stronger and even more resilient. They also recorded that they were better able to see possibilities for the future, relate to others and appreciate life.

> Resilience is associated with realistic optimism, not the rose-coloured form. Because the latter often involves ignoring negative information, people who adopt an overly buoyant outlook tend to underestimate stressful and risky situations. On the other hand, realistic optimists filter out unnecessary negative information but pay close attention to bad news that is relevant to dealing with adversity.
>
> (Southwick and Charney, 2013, pp. 38-39)

This is not always an easy process, but reducing stress will help considerably. Moving from a single inviolate story to considering a range of possibilities will reduce the possibility of you becoming trapped in the narrative. The option of being locked in a bitter of self-denigratory account of events is a dark and distorting venue. Realistic Optimism, however, could lead us to the point where we decide to withdraw from a particular situation. Excessive and unanchored optimism is likely to leave our ashes in the smouldering ruin of a given project or activity.

Social network: A particularly effective way to increase our individual resilience is to maintain a wide-ranging and supportive social network. Please note that these are not virtual friendships! Having a high level of social support has been associated with better psychological outcomes from many types of trauma, including childhood sexual abuse and even the horrors of warfare. In a 1998 study by King *et al* it was found that returning war veterans who maintained a good social network had significantly lower levels of stress and suffered less from post-traumatic stress disorder than did isolates.

The same findings have been found in a wide range of disparate social groupings, including: college students, new mothers, parents of children with serious illnesses, widows and unemployed workers. Knowing that you are backed by others is powerful because it supports self-esteem and personal confidence and is a life-line if we slip. People with a secure social network demonstrate higher levels of self-belief and as a consequence will be more likely to engage actively in problem-solving.

Emotional turbulence: Significant life events are inevitable, though some people appear to believe that their emotions are Teflon-coated and that they will not be impacted by these. The list of these events is considerable: death of a parent, the birth of a child, divorce, ill health, moving to a new house or flat, changing your job, a child leaving home, change in your financial status, getting a speeding ticket, or changing your job. It is important to reflect on the impact of these and not underestimate the effect that they can have. My own mother was 85 when she died; I was 55 and married with three children and working as an education consultant. As a family, we enjoyed good relationships with my mother, who lived nearby. She had a relatively short but serious illness before her death. I rationalised her death as timely. Well you can fill in the clichés. With the value of hindsight I believe that I seriously underestimated the impact of such a significant life event.

When facing bereavement – or indeed, in any of the other situations that I have listed – your resilience will be recalibrated. If we suspect that this is happening, it is advisable to seek help through using a good coach or an appropriate counsellor. Certainly, 'Time is a great healer', but an awful lot can happen while you are waiting.

Good role models: A number of writers have written about the importance of learning through the medium of having and observing appropriate role models. These include Bandura (1963) and it is also a mainstay of Neuro-Linguistic Programming (NLP). Bandura advocated a social learning theory, where he argued that new behaviours can be acquired by observing and imitating others. He stated that learning is a cognitive process and takes place in a social context, and, further, that it can take place purely through observation without direct instruction. Also important in this context is his concept that the observer can learn through the observation of rewards and punishments experienced by those in view, a process known as vicarious reinforcement.

If we apply Bandura's theory to developing our own resilience, then we need to identify people who model resilience. Because there is a downtime with resilience – that is, there are periods in people's lives when resilience is not being called for – it is suggested that you select about six people for your watching brief. It is likely that someone out of the six will be passing through the sort of context where resilience will be required. The target group do not all have to be drawn from teaching. It is not clandestine, it does not require camouflage and binoculars. It is useful to develop an authentic relationship with these people and develop this relationship to the point where you can not only observe without stalking them but be able to discuss their situation and their responses without embarrassment.

If you set your strategy for developing your own resilience within the wider context of stress reduction, then by using the techniques explained throughout this book you will be surprised at how resilience develops. This is not a nicety, but rather it is the right platform from which to advance both your personal and professional lives.

Benefit fraud

The concept of resilience is hard to define and yet it is increasingly understood as being a core trait to be taught to pupils and to be secured amongst teaching staff. Day *et al* concluded:

> It is clear that resilience is a multi-faceted and unstable construct. Its nature and sustainability throughout teachers' different professional life phases will be determined by the interaction between the strength of the vocation of individual teachers, those whom they meet as part of their daily work and the collective resilience of the organisation in its internal and external environments. Their capacities to manage unanticipated, as well as anticipated, events effectively will be mediated by these.
>
> (2011, pp. 26-27)

Perhaps it is its perceived erosion that is highlighting the desirability of resilience as a trait. Like many aspects of human personality that are a synthesis of nature and nurture, the weighting of causality underlying resilience is difficult to establish. For leaders and teachers, workload and the unreasonable expectations that they believe are being imposed on them impact professional sustainability. Arguably, the children that we work with also have emergent problems with resilience. Many are excessively protected in early childhood and then move rapidly to inhabit a digital world where failure and disaster can be resolved by a reset.

The often amorphous characterisation of resilience has opened the door to an opportunistic industry. While many training providers are well intentioned, not all are well informed. Some courses that claim to build individual resilience lack a clear understanding of what it is, and their offer is largely reworked stress reduction products. David Jarvis (2017) writing in *The Telegraph* reported that the Leigh Academies Trust in Kent was making electric shock treatment available to combat anxiety and depression. These machines clearly lack the 'bite' of traditional Electro Convulsive Therapy used in hospital settings. However, their use raises more questions than answers. Certainly, I would want to know how their use is monitored. Are such machines being handed out to staff with pre-existent mental health issues? The use of the 'full-fat' version is contraindicated for pregnancy and driving – is this juvenile version safe in such circumstances? The Royal College of Psychiatrists (R. Barnes, 2015) have stated that the manner in which ECT works is not known and yet a non-medically qualified academy chain has decided to make this available to their staff.

Perhaps the biggest question of all for the Leigh Academy Trust and also for others involved in crafting and leading our education system is 'What is happening in schools and academies that requires intervention with large numbers of teaching staff to ameliorate anxiety and depression?'.

> Human beings are not designed to perform at the outer reaches of endurance on a continual basis. They need ups and downs, excitement and rest. Driving themselves– to work at out all the time leads to breakdown and collapse. Today's uncivilized workplace culture of constant pressure and overwork can only continue at the cost of rising health problems and increasing numbers of people facing a warped and debilitating existence. A workplace needs to meet certain standards to be judged civilized.
>
> (Savage, 2006, p. 9)

Developing strategies to secure personal resilience is beneficial. If you are committing yourself to something that you believe will enhance your wellbeing and that is supported by sound evidence then this is a reasonable action to take. If, however, the initiative is at the behest of your employer and stands within the context of an excessively demanding culture then it is also reasonable to challenge the motivation behind its introduction. It is important to be clear that you are not being offered the equivalent of Coyote's steel helmet. It is suggested that all personal development initiatives should always be offered on the basis of opt in rather than requiring individuals to opt out.

Thinking aloud: it is just possible that we have confused the idea of resilience with that of endurance.

12. A TOUCH OF THE LEONARDOS

It had long since come to my attention that people of accomplishment rarely sat back and let things happen to them. They went out and happened to things.

(Leonardo da Vinci)

Leonardo da Vinci, the 16th-century polymath, excelled in so many areas: invention, mathematics, painting, architecture, geology, astronomy, sculpture, anatomy, literature, botany and engineering. Gardner *et al* argue that he epitomises the Renaissance man with his exploration of so many fields and commented that 'his mind and personality seem to us superhuman, while the man himself, mysterious and remote' (1970, p. 456). As leaders, we may be distanced from Leonardo by degree but certainly not by function. A prime dimension of the role of leadership is to be creatively competent.

Flashes of brilliance

Great ideas are often birthed in a moment and often in unusual places. One of the most famous accounts of a 'flash of brilliance' concerns the 19th-century chemist, August Kekule. A staple of organic chemistry that has led to the development of plastics, pharmaceuticals and supported our study of physiology is the way that the element carbon can provide a skeleton for very complex chemicals such as DNA. One problem that had challenged chemists for a number of years was how the element carbon bonded to form rings as in the case of the compound benzene. Kekule proposed a theory to explain how benzene was structured and in turn facilitated the development of a whole new branch of organic chemistry. This was extremely important for both pure and applied chemistry. In 1890, 25 years after his discovery, he was honoured by The German Chemical Society (Vederese and Roth, 2011). Kekule spoke at this meeting of how he derived his ground-breaking theory. He related that he had discovered the ring shape of the benzene molecule after having a day-dream of a snake seizing its own tail. This 'dream' included visualising an ancient symbol known as the ouroboros, which depicts a snake or serpent eating its own tail. He suggested that this vision was rooted in his long-term study of the nature of carbon-carbon bonds.

There is a long line of such discoveries: Archimedes leaping from his bath and developing the idea of specific gravity; Sir Timothy Berners-Lee's conceptualisation of the world wide web; Sir Alexander Fleming's discovery of Penicillin; and even Albert Einstein's theory of relativity, which he conceived whilst riding a bike. These are inspirational stories, though some are mired in urban mythology. However, what does become clear is that significant creative thinking often happens as 'flashes of brilliance'. Of course, the execution of these ideas can then take considerable effort and planning.

Earley *et al* (2011) conducted research into the experiences of newly appointed headteachers working in urban environments. I undertook some of the field research and interviewed some of these headteachers who contributed to the research. A number spoke of how they often came up with solutions to vexatious problems when they were doing repetitive or isolated tasks. They spoke of cycling, running and even being in the shower as providing seminal moments for coming up with solutions to problems that they saw as being challenging. This book (and here I open myself up to potential criticism) was conceived both in terms of its overall theme and even a lot of its content whilst driving home late one night between the Fleet and Winchester Services on the M3 motorway.

Significant thinking often seems to require us to occupy a particular space and adopt a high level of focus. Many hypnotherapists would describe this as a state of trance. This often-misunderstood term relates to a state of inward focus or reflection where external and internal distractions have been dialled down.

Interestingly, at the time of writing, the use of drugs Ritalin, Modafinil and Adderall are being reported as being used quite widely in universities to support such thinking.

> Gemma, 26, works in the City of London, where stakes are high and hours are long. She is also coming to the end of her part-time masters. And dissertation deadline day is looming. 'I was finding it really hard to engage in study when I got home, after working from 9*am* to 7*pm* or later,' she told Channel 4 News. 'I was panicking in quite a big way.'

> Gemma remembered a friend, who studied at UCL a few years ago, talking about how Ritalin had helped towards the end of her course: 'Her and her friends said you just become incredibly focused. She jokingly said: "I spent seven hours formatting a graph".'

> (Ritchie, 2013)

There is a growing interest in chemically induced focus with these powerful drugs being obtained from friends who have been prescribed them (probably for a condition such as ADHD) or by ordering them online. It is not the intention of this book to recommend the use of such drugs to achieve focus and its sustention. Indeed, there is emerging evidence that taking these drugs on a regular basis can adversely affect the brain chemistry:

> We saw changes in the brain chemistry in ways that are known to have an impact on the reward pathway, locomotor activity, and other behaviors, as well as effects on body weight. These changes in brain chemistry were associated with serious concerns such as risk-taking behaviors, disruptions in the sleep/wake cycle and problematic weight loss, as well as resulting in increased activity and anti-anxiety and antidepressive effects.
>
> (Panayotis, 2017)

This somewhat deviant route to enhanced concentration confirms the view that creative and demanding tasks do require high levels of focus and that the execution of the output from this thinking will require sustained commitment to bringing the ideas(s) to reality. The point has already been made that adverse stress – distress – is a biological defence mechanism with the function of narrowing options and switching body preparedness to physical response. This is the polar opposite to the requirements of supporting creativity. The latter is about considering a wide range of options and connecting to a broad and diverse flow of information. So again, creativity is facilitated by a reduction in stress and interruption. It is further enhanced by using techniques such as brainstorming that enhance multiple options and possibilities.

This conclusion mirrors that of the work of the influential psychologist Mihalyi Csikszentmihalyi. He wrote his ground-breaking *Flow: The Psychology of Optimal Experience* in 1990. He described people who are totally absorbed in a task as being in a state of flow. At this juncture, nothing else appears to matter to the person. This state of flow has sometimes been described as being 'in the zone' or even by the rather archaic expression as being 'in the groove'. We have all experienced this and enjoyed that feeling of great absorption, engagement, fulfilment, and the use of skills. Issues such as time, thoughts about ourselves, even hunger and thirst do not intrude. Every thought follows sequentially with your whole being involved. Perhaps most importantly, your skills are being used to the utmost and your mental processes are aligned. Flow, as a concept, connects in a number of ways with mindfulness, though they differ significantly in that mindfulness does not have an explicit focus, rather its preoccupation with, for example, breathing as a means to an end. It can be a precursor to creative thinking.

Where a flow state is being achieved there will be a balance between the challenge of the task and the skills of the individual. If the task lacks challenge by being too easy, or if it is excessively daunting, then flow will not occur. The maxim for all learning is 'high skill and high challenge'. If there is a lack of challenge then apathy will be the almost inevitable consequence, if there is a lack of appropriate skills then the challenge will induce anxiety.

Csikszentmihalyi has also explored motivation and became interested in what he came to term the 'autotelic personality'. This personality type is one in which a person performs acts because they are intrinsically rewarding, rather than to achieve external goals.

> An autotelic person needs few material possessions and little entertainment, comfort, power, or fame because so much of what he or she does is already rewarding. Because such persons experience flow in work, in family life, when interacting with people, when eating, even when alone with nothing to do, they are less dependent on the external rewards that keep others motivated to go on with a life composed of routines. They are more autonomous and independent because they cannot be as easily manipulated with threats or rewards from the outside. At the same time, they are more involved with everything around them because they are fully immersed in the current of life.
>
> (Csikszentmihalyi, 1997, p. 117)

Whilst excessive stereotyping is not helpful, it may well be that such personality types will incline towards unfettered curiosity and find themselves detached from management imperatives. Other personality types could emphasise the completion of managerial tasks.

If only it was that simple

The activity of leadership is multifaceted and yet frequently these different dimensions are not given sufficient consideration by practitioners. There is a fork in the road between problem-solving and the development of vision. Arguably they can both involve creativity but they are subtly different. Heifetz *et al* (2009) argued that there are two types of change: adaptive and technical. A given 'technical change' may be demanding but its hallmark is that the problem can be identified, a solution proposed and a resolution implemented. Adaptive change, so Heifetz argues, is typified by an issue or problem which has no common agreed diagnosis and for which there is no agreed solution.

Education defies both definition and solution; there really is no best fit. Frequently, simplistic metrics are used to identify limited outcomes. Not surprisingly, Heifetz's work on adaptive leadership has become a focus of interest in education as well as in the business and commercial world. This approach to leadership and change will usually require collaborative thinking and importantly collective learning in order to achieve good outcomes. This approach does not negate the role of the individual leader in engaging with creativity. Rather, it requires the leader to take the role of the conductor and draw the whole ensemble into creating a memorable performance whilst engaging with their insights and ideas. There is no requirement for the conductor to play all the instruments. Such a role requires profound individual reflection as a prelude to collaborative interpretation.

The role of leadership

The role of the leader could be defined by the answer to the question, 'What I am doing today?'. Leadership is very much a 'Swiss Army Knife' of a profession, with a blade for everything. Leaders are in the centre of a vortex of demands and also work in a context which can be both turbulent, unpredictable and demanding. It was Dwight D Eisenhower, a former US president, who reputedly organised his workload and priorities using the following matrix:

	Urgent	Not urgent
Important	Urgent and important	Not urgent but important
Not important	Urgent but not important	Not urgent and not important

Table 12.0 Decision making matrix (Attributed to the American President Dwight D Eisenhower)

This diagram will be familiar to many:

- **Urgent and important** – this is very much the dimension of management, the task of 'making today happen'.

- **Important and not urgent** – this is the dimension concerned with leadership. This is the category where strategy and vision are birthed.

111

- **Urgent but not important** – perhaps rather cynically, this is the area of activity that largely becomes dictated by others.

- **Not urgent and not important** – a little of this can bring respite from pressure but if this is where you live as a leader then it is unlikely that you will be leading for much longer.

Of course, creative solutions are needed for managerial problems but creativity comes into its own when we engage with the 'important and not urgent'. Action in this area can be delayed but these tasks cannot be deferred indefinitely. Leadership connects with action and direction and it can never be a magical mystery tour.

It is essential that we plan to think without interruption, setting up our headspace to operate at its most powerful. You may choose to work with others, but again this has to be carefully managed with each contributor aware of their responsibility in supporting excellence.

Many leaders experience considerable guilt if they take time out to think. Actually, they should feel guilty if they do not.

13. HEADSPACE

The trouble is, the modern work paradigm gives us so little sense of completion or clear space that it feels like we're constantly straining to see the light at the end of a long, long tunnel.

(Allcott, 2016, p. 5)

I was fascinated by a colleague's office. Every surface, including the floor, was covered with stacks of paper. There were curriculum materials, policy documents, correspondence, students' work and even various hobby-related magazines. It was spectacular, like the Manhattan skyline modelled in print. Because he never threw anything away, he was always a good source for an elusive set of minutes or the departmental budget from five years earlier. It was intriguing how easily he could locate a document from what appeared to be a totally random pile. In the interest of transparency, I do need to confess that I also had a malicious desire to see one of these stacks collapse rather in the style of the latter phase of a game of Jenga.

His computer ran on similar principles with over 14000 emails in his inbox. His wallpaper picture of his family was obscured by huge numbers documents stored on his desktop.

Over time, my sense of awe at his ability to abstract information (and even his ability to walk from one side of his office to the other) faded. I realised that his amazing feats were inappropriate and that maintaining an index of the contents of his disordered lifestyle was using up a significant amount of his headspace. Allen draws the analogy between the way the brain processes information and the RAM of a computer and argues:

Everything you've told yourself you ought to do, your mind thinks you should do right now. Frankly, as soon as you have two things to do stored in your RAM, you've generated personal failure, because you can't do two things at the same time. This produces an all-pervasive stress factor whose source can't be pin-pointed.

(2001, p. 23)

Writers such as Allen (2001), Kustenmacher (2004) and Allcott (2016) have changed the debate from scheduling your work tasks to creating the conditions for optimal thinking. In a knowledge economy, leaders, like many others, are employed to think creatively and not rent out their heads to store information.

Getting a quart into a pint pot
(1.13652 litres into a 0.568261-litre pot in new money)

It is a statement of the obvious that we only have 24 hours each day at our disposal. We can juggle activities in the short term by borrowing against our sleep or family time, but ultimately we will have to repay that loan.

The evolution of many time-management systems is largely predicated on the concept of breaking available time down into packets alongside an established ranked order of priorities. One of the earliest was Filofax (literally a 'file of facts') and it has its origins with a notebook issued to infantry officers in World War I. The Covey organisation has drawn, to some extent, upon the Eisenhower Matrix as the basis of their time-management system which uses a raft of grids and templates.

These are useful tools, but at heart they remain very much tools of management by creating schedules and space to complete a range of managerial tasks, making today happen. Their limitations become apparent if you use one of these systems to try and schedule a block of time for creative thinking or for solving wicked problems. This state will not respond well to being brought into play within a specific time-slot. This has led to different approaches – notably that of Allen (2001), where he develops a methodology for getting information, half-formed ideas, action plans and commitments, from all areas of our lives, out of our heads into a supportive system. The mental space created then becomes fertile ground for germinating ideas. He suggests three foundational principles:

First of all, if it's on your mind, your mind isn't clear. Anything you consider unfinished in any way must be captured in a trusted system outside your mind, or what I call a collection bucket, that you know you'll come back to regularly and sort through.

Second, you must clarify exactly what your commitment is and decide what you have to do, if anything, to make progress toward fulfilling it.

> Third, once you've decided on all the actions you need to take, you must keep reminders of them organised in a system you review regularly.
>
> (2001, p. 13)

This paradigm shift expressed by the likes of Allen (2001), Kustenmacher (2004) and Allcott (2016) is not about their advocacy of a particular system of organising and scheduling but rather their articulation of the intention of the process. All of them chart a way to get organised; however, the consequent success is not dependent on a given app, template or programme. It is primarily about developing a system that clears information, actions *etc* out of the head. The acid test is that if you are following their approach and find yourself running a neural back up in addition to your external ones, then there is a need to make significant modifications to your system. If you do not have complete trust in your system, then (so it is argued) you will not gain the intended benefits.

> Be sure that you're not forgetting important items by keeping all of your support information in a system, not in your head. Be sure that you're not distracted and stressed by what you could be forgetting – by using a second brain instead of your head as the place where information and reminders live. This is certainly easier said than done, but once mastered, really works.
>
> (Allcott, 2016, p. 12)

It is worth remembering that even the humble filing system has always been about action and not archive.

The power of no

Saying 'Yes' to a request is almost certainly overused. Frequently, we say yes because of emotional pressure, perhaps a desire to be accepted or liked and sometimes it just feels like an easier option. With the benefit of later reflection, we, often conclude that we have made the wrong response. However, responding to such requests with 'No', even though we have tactfully packaged it, causes many people to feel uneasy and even guilty. An additional contribution to our anxiety is the baggage of negativity that has come to be associated with the word. When people say 'No', they feel that they have slammed the door in another's face.

Responding to a request with an unequivocal 'Yes' can have a lot of power: *it can support team work, communicate affirmation,* risk-taking, courage and a generous approach to life and others. Saying 'No' is seldom celebrated. If we are going to prioritise the creation of 'headspace', then 'No' will have to become more prominent in our vocabulary.

The confusion that exists between declining a request and the perception that we are being negative often means that we lose out on the empowerment that its considered use can bring. They can be seen as being superficially similar; however, they are very different psychological states. Sills highlights this difference:

> Negativity is a chronic attitude, a pair of emotional glasses through which some people get a cloudy view of the world. Negativity expresses itself in a whining perfectionism, a petulant discontent, or risk-averse naysaying.

It's an energy sapper. Negative people may douse the enthusiasm of others, but rarely inspire them to action. Negativity certainly ensures that you will not be pleased. You will also not be powerful.

(2013, p. 26)

'No' is about making a choice and transcending the conflicting feelings running through your head. As such, using the response can be a moment of personal clarity and empowerment. It is both the means and the boundary marker by which we establish and maintain the distinct perimeter of who we are and what we do. It is not about making a statement of dissociation or being difficult, rather it is about being clear about our capabilities, capacity and values in a more explicit format than repeatedly saying 'Yes' will secure.

Too many times, I have said 'Yes' to a request and then subsequently regretted and even resented the stress that acquiescing has generated. My headspace had now been caught in a pincer movement of concerns over time pressures and also a reduction in my self-esteem because yet again I have given in. In Chapter 3, there is a brief outline of the Drama or Karpman Triangle. Forrest (2008) highlights a series of commonly occurring preferred starting points when we engage with conversations. If your most common point of engagement is what was referred to as a 'starting gate rescuer' then you will have some significant work to undertake to get out of the 'Yes' trap. If we tend to capitulate to the requests or manipulation of others we need to break free from that resonance.

GR1

I attended a research meeting where I work. The lead for the project, a respected academic, was clearly somewhat distracted. It transpired that, the previous day, she had decided to defrost her freezer and discovered that if you use a kitchen knife as your tool of choice, you can puncture the coolant carrying tubes and release the refrigerant gas. The research meeting soon developed a somewhat surreal quality as we worked on our research methodology, interspaced by phone conversations with a refrigeration engineer and a discussion as to whether to mend or replace the damaged appliance. The engineer's response was tinged with some reluctance as the damaged freezer was on the sixth floor of a block of flats. It was fascinating how this domestic mishap had grabbed a piece of my colleague's headspace and how much it was derailing our meeting.

Each of our possessions lays claim to a fraction of our head. In most cases, this is fairly negligible. On the other hand, the impact of some of our material possessions can extremely intrusive. If you own an older car, just think for a moment how anxious you can become before the MOT; or alternatively, consider how stressed people become when their broadband fails.

This set a train of thinking departing from my mental station and I decided to cull my material possessions. This was not envisaged as being extreme, but rather more at the 'life's laundry' end of the spectrum. I implemented 'GR1' (Get Rid of 1 Thing Every Day). I recorded each item that I sold on Gumtree, gave away, took to a charity shop and even those that went to the tip. Some items were large, such as the two unwanted bikes I sold; while some were small, like the read detective novel that went to the charity shop. Of course, it is important not to become obsessional or you will create a new preoccupation which would have the potential to eclipse the impact of the clutter and even leave you sitting on the floor.

I have done this for six months and it has been astonishing how much I have got rid of. This is about clutter and not essentials or memorabilia, it is not about becoming 'hair shirt' over possessions. However, alongside the obvious reduction in the unnecessary items that were filling my life, the process has felt quite cathartic. It has also reduced the casual purchase of further items. On mentioning GR1 to a few friends, some have decided to try it and their feedback has been unanimously positive.

The head does not have a loft for the storage of clutter. Everything is present in one space, our headspace.

Decongestant

This chapter has not been about developing a better filing system, though that might be an outcome. It is not even about taking on board a time-management system or transferring from a paper system to a digital one. Older style time-management systems tend to emphasise management rather than leadership. Such approaches are very much linked to making today happen rather than about conceptualising a future and helping others journey towards that vision.

It is about selecting systems that appeal to you and that you have absolute confidence and trust in so that you can think in a creative and undistracted manner. The systems you select are there to facilitate just this. We need to ensure that the servant does not inadvertently become the master as you juggle a complex app that has offered the claim that you will become more productive. Many time-management approaches simply oil the bearings on the hamster wheel, whereas our task is to get out of the cage.

It's almost banal to allude to the rapid changes in our world: globalisation, competition for resources, loss of national identity, the knowledge explosion with its attendant technologies, people migration, changing patterns in our employment and the need for personal strategies to remain as lifelong learners. This is before the next big waves break as we face the implications of the

Internet of Things and Artificial Intelligence. Into this bewildering mix our education system is tending to become more rigid, drawing inspiration from the past rather than the future. There is a need to liberate leadership from task so that it can be invited to shape new modes and pathways of education. There is a need for leaders who have headspace to innovate. It is hard to see the stars when you are bent down tying your shoelaces.

14. DIGIFREE

If the only way you could read an email was to run a mile first, the urge would quickly die. Human beings constantly do subconscious effort/ reward calculations. Tapping a screen is the easiest of physical tasks.

(Dr Andrew Weil)

In 2008, I wrote the unintended prequel to this book, *The Constant Leader*. One chapter was entitled 'Tool to Tyrant' (pp. 57-61) and dealt with the overwhelming experience many leaders face in coping with a 24/7, connected work environment. It was packed with practical advice on managing the information flow and creating boundaries between ourselves and this interconnected and free-flowing medium. The tenor of the chapter was that information exchange had changed up several gears and that we would have to adapt our existing practice to stay in the game. In the last few years, I have increasingly moved from dealing with input to considering the impact of digital immersion.

Ten years on from writing that book, information technology has increased in both speed and capacity. The industry has created a new range of platforms that have extended our engagement with digital devices. My perspective has altered and I argue that our digital substrate is far less benign than we had previously thought. Of course, the argument is not that we become latter-day Luddites. I for one would not wish to return to that heady amalgam of the mechanical typewriter, Tipp-Ex and carbon paper or make international phone calls interrupted by an anxious parent gesticulating about the cost. However, as we fete ICT's Dr Jekyll, there is a need to reflect on his shadow alter-ego, Mr Hyde.

Mr Hyde's computer

A visit to a high street betting shop will bring you face-to-face with the 'Fixed Odds Betting Terminal' (FOBT). Introduced in 2001, these terminals allow players to bet on the outcome of various games with fixed odds, such as roulette. They raise astonishing amounts of revenue for their owners; in 2016, it was £1.8 billion pounds in the UK alone (Davies, 2017). Behind these takings is a string of tragic stories of individuals who have lost homes, families and jobs as they gambled as much as £100 every 20 seconds.

By now you are probably thinking that this argument has become somewhat tangential. However, the link lies in understanding the design of these machines and its relationship with the way that we interact with our own digital devices. FOBTs are skilfully designed using psychological insights to draw individuals into their maw. A *Guardian* editorial argues:

> FOBTs trade on a psychological insight: what keeps customers engaged is less the hope of winning than the pleasure of playing. They are designed to induce a state of 'flow', or being 'in the zone', in which all of the player's attention and consciousness is pulled into the game, and nothing from the outside world can impinge. It is, while it lasts, entirely satisfying. This is a similar mechanism to that which, in popular myth at least, leads teenagers, lost in their video games, to starve to death after playing for days and nights without sleep or food. It depends on speed of play, and infrequent but never predictable rewards. The knowledge that intermittent reinforcement works better than predictable rewards goes back to the psychologist BF Skinner's theory of conditioning, and the gaming industry takes full advantage of it.
>
> (*The Guardian*, 2017b)

Underlying such fast and repetitious reward processes is the brain's dopamine system. In conditioning, the action is rewarded with the release of euphoria-inducing neurotransmitters, notably dopamine. The latter is released to encourage us to repeat life-sustaining activities such as eating healthy food, having sex, drinking water, and remaining in nurturing relationships. It is intended to operate within the context of healthy relationships and lifestyles. However, it can become detached and provide the springboard for developing damaging addictions such as overeating, drug and alcohol abuse, consumerism and, of course, gambling.

So let us take a step back from the world of Paddy Power, Coral or Ladbrokes and return to our digital world. This same physiology drives our engagement with our laptops, smartphones and tablets. Many people routinely spread their attention across emails, texts, Instagram, Facebook, Pinterest, Snapchat and Twitter and many others. In many cases, it is not simply about choosing a social medium of choice but trying for a blanket coverage across a number, perhaps, as many as five or six.

If you are committed to maintaining a presence on social media then you will face two immediate pressures and a further potential one. Firstly, you will come under pressure to maintain the flow of your material and secondly your brain will become stimulated by an expectation of a response. While a lack of response can be disappointing, it is suggested that immediate or near-immediate responses can be more damaging. They position you squarely within the stimulus-response loop that is generating repetition by the release of dopamine. This is not so different from the person playing the FOBTs.

The potential risk is from adverse or critical comment which can be very damaging as people make abusive comments from an anonymous distance. Comments that they would never make in a face to face context.

It is not uncommon for people who are unable to access or check their smartphones on a regular basis to display similar levels of stress as those seen in deprived smokers or drinkers. It is important to recognise that such behaviour is not about breaches of etiquette but it is actually evidence of dopamine-driven addictive behaviour.

The smartphone, our most portable digital device, is amazing in its capability and capacity. It can, of course, be used as a phone or to text, to calculate, to find addresses, access the internet, measure your exercise, get a weather forecast, track a friend, set your alarm, listen to music, diagnose medical conditions, construct to-do lists, play games *etc*. Its power exceeds mainframe computers in use even 30 years ago whilst it is almost impossible to compare one with Bletchley Park's Colossus Mk 2, built in 1944. This ran on 2400 valves. In contrast, we can use our smartphone on the move and, because of its versatility, it will draw us into some level of multitasking. We check Twitter whilst queuing, listen to music as we walk, connect to 24/7 rolling news as we eat and check what our friends are doing or saying even as we hold a face-to-face conversation with others.

Miller, a neuroscientist at the Massachusetts Institute of Technology, employs strong language when he refers to our alleged ability to multitask as a 'powerful and diabolical illusion'. One of the world's leading experts on divided attention, he states unequivocally:

> Our brains are not wired to multitask well ... When people think they're multitasking, they're actually just switching from one task to another very rapidly. And every time they do, there's a cognitive cost in doing so.
>
> (2013, p.3)

He argues that we are not expert jugglers able to maintain a lot of balls in the air at once but, rather, that we are more like bad 'plate-spinners' rushing from one task to another and ignoring the one in front in order to give attention to others. This frantic activity is not the index of our productivity; in fact, the more diverse things that we do concurrently, the less efficient we become.

Any form of multitasking will increase the level of the stress hormones cortisol and adrenaline in our bodies. Acting in tandem, these can overstimulate the brain and generate brain fog or disaggregate our thinking. Miller (2013) also argues that multitasking creates and sustains this dopamine-addiction feedback loop, which actually rewards the brain for losing focus. The prefrontal cortex is enchanted with the new and will easily allow the brain to redirect its focus and attention towards novelty. We are the ultimate cognitive jackdaws. Levitin, another neuroscientist, states:

> We answer the phone, look up something on the internet, check our email, send an SMS, and each of these things tweaks the novelty-seeking, reward-seeking centres of the brain, causing a burst of endogenous opioids (no wonder it feels so good!), all to the detriment of our staying on task. It is the ultimate empty-caloried brain candy. Instead of reaping the big rewards that come from sustained, focused effort, we instead reap empty rewards from completing a thousand little sugar-coated tasks.
>
> (2015, p. 1)

It gets worse! Ward *et al* (2017) found that cognitive capacity is significantly reduced when a person's smartphone is within reach, even if it is turned off. In their study, 800 smartphone users where asked to complete a series of tests on a computer. These were designed to require full concentration in order for an individual to achieve high scores. The tests were geared to measure participants' available cognitive capacity – the brain's ability to hold and process data at any given time. All participants were asked to turn their phones to silent. Some of the participants were randomly instructed to place their phones either next to them but face down, in a pocket or in a bag, while others were asked to leave their phones in another room.

The research project showed that where a participant had left their phone in another room they significantly outperformed the group who had their phones on the desk beside them. They, also, albeit slightly, outperformed those who had their phones in a pocket, briefcase or handbag. The findings suggest that the mere presence of our smartphone reduces our available cognitive capacity and impairs our cognitive functioning, despite the fact that we believe that we are giving the task in hand our full attention. When interviewed by Fotalia about his findings, Ward suggested that:

> As the smartphone becomes more noticeable, participants' available cognitive capacity decreases … Your conscious mind isn't thinking about your smartphone, but that process – the process of requiring yourself to not think about something – uses up some of your limited cognitive resources. It's a brain drain.
>
> (Fotalia, 2017, p. 1)

Ward and his team (2017) extended their reach in a further experiment. They looked at how an individual's self-assessed dependence on their smartphone mapped against cognitive capacity. The same series of computer-based tasks were used to assess performance. Again, participants were asked to switch their phones off and then randomly given similar locations to store them while the participants took the tests.

The research findings indicated that the higher the level of dependency on the digital device of the participant, the worse the participant performed in the tests. However, putting the phone in an adjacent room restored the levels of their performance. The conclusion was that having your smartphone within sight or within easy reach actually reduces your ability to focus and perform tasks because part of your brain is actively working to ignore the phone.

Take note

Increasingly, people are taking notes on their laptop. It seems to be self-evident that it is useful to keep as much as possible in one central location. However, recent research by Mueller and Oppenheimer (2014) suggest that taking notes by hand initiates a different style of cognitive processing than when notes are being taken using a laptop. Writing by hand is obviously slower than typing. However, the long-hand notetaker appears to compensate by exhibiting higher levels of listening and then summarise the key points of the material more effectively. The process of manually transcribing a presentation or meeting into note form seems to support both comprehension and also retention. The use of a laptop appears to result in a somewhat shallow and even mindless capture of information. The higher level of verbatim notetaking derived from using a laptop in this way was associated with lower rates of retention.

Even when students were warned of these potential dangers, there was no recorded change in either the manner of the laptop-based notetaking or in levels of retention. It is suggested that because longhand notes contain the notetaker's own words, these may also connect more effectively with their memory.

Digital dream

When the importance of sleep was considered in Chapter 9, 'Nightshift', mention was made of the control mechanisms that regulate our sleep and wakefulness. There is a central 'biological clock' (circadian clock) which largely controls this pattern, but other factors come into play. Light has a significant role to play. Falling asleep in a brightly lit room is difficult because the light is stimulating particular cells in the retinas of our eyes and suppressing the secretion of the sleep-inducing hormone melatonin.

LED digital screens and also low energy light bulbs can adversely affect the functioning of the circadian clock because they produce particular wavelengths of light which are more likely to suppress the production of melatonin. LED screens are backlit and emit high levels of melatonin-inhibiting blue light and less of the sleep-supporting yellow frequencies. Perhaps it is back to the book at bedtime, maybe with a cup of Horlicks?

Plan to think

This chapter appears to come out as 3-0 to the Luddites. Well perhaps not! It is clearly unreasonable to become a sort of IT version of King Canute. However, I would suggest that there is sufficient research to challenge or at least cause us to review our use of digital devices. Key roles for the leader will include solving problems, creating strategic direction, evaluating progress and facilitating the forward momentum of the organisation. These are complex and certainly higher-order cognitive skills. Impairment, because we are being inhibited by the unregulated use of digital technology, cannot be argued as being likely to stack the odds in our favour.

So, five interventions to regulate your digital environment in order enhance your thinking:

- Use digital devices purposefully. Schedule times when you will be available to use them and do not let them become interwoven with real conversations or creative thinking. My boss for a number of years is a red wine enthusiast. To keep his hobby in check he has followed the medical advice of having two days of abstention. Could this be a useful strategy to use with smartphones? Strangely, these abstinence days have never coincided with occasions when we have gone out for a meal.

- When undertaking extended tasks such as change projects, budgets or development plans, turn off your emails and leave your phone in another room. It is worth remembering that after being interrupted it can take about 25 minutes to get back to where you left off and that is after only a 2.8-second interruption. Error and tiredness are other negative consequences.

- Clear your bedroom of digital devices and remember their primary purpose. Leave your smartphone/tablet downstairs and do not use it as an alarm clock. In fact, buy a dedicated alarm clock with a switchable display.

- Put a signature on your emails stating the times when you will be accessing them. *De facto*, this should include the weekends. I am working towards automatically deleting all emails that arrive in my inbox over a weekend. That has certainly challenged me to think about my own stance on this issue.

- Consider reducing your presence on social media and reduce your time playing games. Recently, one friend apologised for not having a smartphone. It is just possible that he is ahead of the curve.

High-quality thinking merits high-quality time that has as its hallmark a lack of interruption. Some will argue that this is an unreasonable expectation. The counter argument is that there is an unacceptably high cost to evolving organisations resulting from poorly structured leadership thinking.

15. BEYOND HELLO

Our work, our relationships, and our lives succeed or fail one conversation at a time. While no single conversation is guaranteed to transform a company, a relationship, or a life, any single conversation can. Speak and listen as if this is the most important conversation you will ever have with this person. It could be. Participate as if it matters. It does.

(Scott, 2002, p. xv)

Leaders do not have casual conversations; there is no dialogic downtime when you are present within the organisation. This is not about trying to use communication to establish a diktat that somehow stands independent of who we are. Pause for a moment and it becomes clear that words that we speak are how we are known or, indeed, not known. Our conversations, our leadership conversations, frame motivation, relationships, change and of course trust.

All conversations have a number of facets and these must all be brought into alignment when we communicate. Mehrabian (1967), famously made the point that:

- 7% of a message pertaining to feelings and attitudes is in the words that are spoken.

- 38% of a message pertaining to feelings and attitudes is paralinguistic (the way that the words are said).

- 55% of a message pertaining to feelings and attitudes is in facial expression.

Unfortunately, his work is frequently misrepresented as it relates to the establishment of rapport or connectedness rather than content or straight meaning. It would be ridiculous to present the school or academy budget to the directors using 'tic-tac' techniques borrowed from racetrack bookmakers. We need rapport because it opens the possibilities for enhanced communication. What is being said still needs to have substance. In some ways, dialogue is similar to an iceberg. There is that which is seen and then significant substance that is below the waterline.

Are you speaking to me?

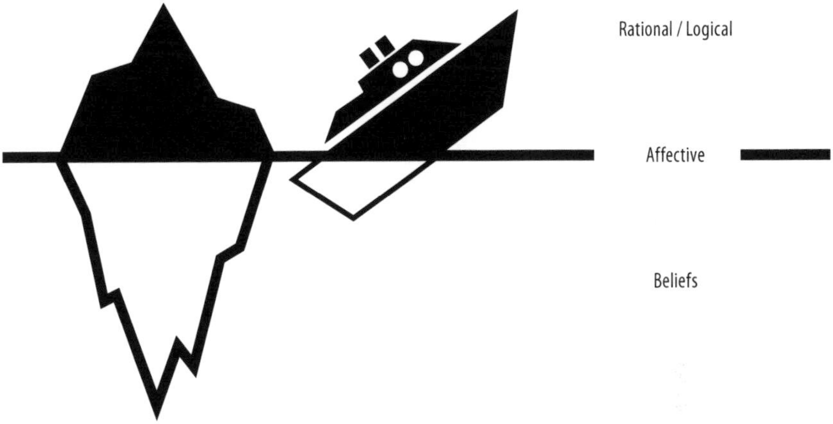

Rational / Logical

Affective

Beliefs

Figure 15.0 Are you speaking to me?

The rational, logical part of the brain is where many of our discussions connect around a significant number of our professional issues. This part of our brain can engage in debate, generate solutions and create and innovate. In relative terms, however, it is dwarfed by what lies below, the limbic system or mid-brain region. There are also our affective or emotional behaviours, which hover around the 'waterline' playing a sort of 'now you see them and now you don't'. The latter can be warm and affirming or drive extreme defensive behaviours forward – for example, anger. Centred in the limbic system are two structures called the amygdala. In case of perceived threat these will initiate an override and commit our resources to survival. These are the structures that can generate road rage. When these are triggered it produces the so called 'amygdala hijack' which tends to last for perhaps 15-20 minutes but can last for much longer. Never reason with an individual in such a state; wait for it to pass.

When we are in dialogue there has to be a connection at every level, this is what is meant by rapport. The emotions play a powerful part in establishing this but so too do other areas of the limbic system which are monitoring movements, tonality and in particular keeping a watching brief for any potential threat. In most conversations, emotional resonance will be established on the basis of who is generating the most powerful emotions. It is a bit like a guitarist playing a note on one guitar and the string on a similarly tuned guitar resonating with it. We do the same with our emotions. There is a danger that when we are faced with a person manifesting powerful emotions, they are more likely to take centre stage and begin to change our own emotional signature in line with theirs. Empowered communication takes place when we can resist the centripetal pull of another person's emotions and begin to override theirs. I would strongly suggest this should be in a positive direction by establishing calm and reducing anxiety. It will work the other way round, but most people do not want to create a hornet-in-a-jam-jar situation!

Routinely, leaders have to have challenging conversations with colleagues. These could well include areas like change-management, giving feedback, and performance issues. We can use our role and authority to package our message but it is a bit like stroking a dog's fur against the grain, in that it will generate resistance and distraction. Professional dialogue should be structured. Do not get lured into or initiate a corridor ambush but arrange for a further conversation to be had in an appropriate context. After all, when I visit the doctors I do not expect to be examined in the health centre waiting room. Rapport is crucial and the physical basis of rapport has already been considered in Chapter 3. The following three points build on this and are offered as the basis of creating positive rapport with another person:

1. Ensure that you are in a state of personal calmness. Our focus must be directed towards the other person and so ensure that we can capture their subtle communication cues. High stress levels will put us on an 'alert status' as we search for potential threat and so we will become attuned to anything which is negative and hostile – or worse, we will recast harmless or objective comments as belonging to this same category. Our stress will almost certainly be picked up by the other person's 'limbic radar'.

2. Understand the other person as being interesting or even intriguing. Rapport is readily built when we want to know more about others, their views and insights. We need to foster an expectation that we will learn from the other person. Rapport comes more from pulling within a conversation than from pushing. If we see others as an audience for our erudition we may find that rapport becomes an elusive commodity.

3. Remember Mehrabian's argument that so much is communicated through non-verbal communication. Work your body language to advantage, consciously mirroring and matching your movements and tonality with the other person. It is useful to remember that the more discordant that non-verbal communication becomes, rapport is diminished and effective communication is attenuated. One caveat

is that if the other person is demonstrating aggressive or agitated behaviour, do not fall into sync with them. Rather, display calm and non-threatening behaviours that will draw the other person into an altogether more constructive frame.

The target here is developing an authentic rapport with the other person. Many of these techniques can and will support effective communication. They can be subverted and honed to become tools of manipulation. Neuro Linguistic Programming (NLP) often plays around the edges of these types of techniques. In our leadership conversations, the other person will probably cope with being presented with a different point of view but almost certainly react badly if we try to manipulate them with spurious techniques and insincerity.

Conversational leadership

A number of writers have recognised conversation as being germane to effective leadership – for example, see the opening quotation from Scott (2002). Other writers have elevated this one-to-one conversational approach to a leadership style in its own right. These include Hurley and Brown (2009), Veenman and Hart (2014) and Groysberg and Slind (2012). Effective communication is clearly desirable within organisations. The Conversational Leadership movement have really used it as a tool to leverage engagement and contribution. This is the coming-together of people to 'think out of the box' and start to tackle those ill-defined 'wicked problems'. There are similarities with Google's 20% time. Employees were let off the leash to think creatively in terms of new thinking that would extend the reach of the company. This radical approach led to the invention of Gmail, Google News and even Adsense. Currently, there is some uncertainty as to whether it is still in existence as pressing commercial pressures have tended to limit the availability of staff to participate. A similar approach was the development of the Results Only Work Environment (ROWE). This Australian-based system focused on results rather than time spent. Collison and Parcel (2001) highlighted the informal knowledge-sharing systems that grew up within BP. Each of these approaches keeps trying to edge the organisational world from a hierarchical system to something much more organic and participative.

Hurley and Brown (2009) provide a good illustrative vignette which shows how this can become a different but positive mode of working. They cite the experience of Bob Veazie, a senior engineer and manufacturing manager at Hewlett Packard. He had been involved in a 'World Café Activity' (see panel over the page).

The World Café

In a World Café conversation, participants are seated in groups of four or five on separate tables. These are laid out much in the style of pavement café with table cloths, vases of flowers and notepads.

Participants explore 'questions that matter', very much dealing with those complex issues where collaboration can make a significant difference to generating solutions.

The 'host', or table facilitator stays on the table as others move on to form other groups. This 'host' shares the headlines from the previous conversation that took place at the table and a new conversation starts. The conversations begin to connect and network and innovation emerges.

Overall, the collective knowledge begins to grow and gain momentum. After several rounds of conversations around one or more of the issues, the participants share their insights, learning and suggestion for action. There is a 'harvest' of the conversations of the whole group.

After participating in the event, Veazie commented:

Something profound but disturbing happened to me during those café conversations. I realized that the boxes on my organization chart might more accurately be depicted as webs of conversations. Each day, we are engaged in conversations about different questions, just like in those table conversations, and we move between the 'tables' as we do our work in the company. It hit me with laser-beam clarity: *This is how life actually works!* So I began to wonder: If our conversations and personal relations are at the heart of our work, how am I, as a leader, contributing to or taking energy away from this natural process? Are we using the intelligence of just a few people when we could gain the intelligence of hundreds or thousands by focusing on key questions and including people more intentionally in the conversation?'

(Hurley and Brown, 2009)

Conversational leadership becomes embedded as an approach when leaders see their organisation less as a hierarchical 'Christmas tree', with themselves as the star on the top, and more as a network where powerful conversations facilitate systemic change. Such an approach inevitably grows intellectual and social capital; it also mirrors and connects with our increasingly networked world.

Conflict

All organisations present their members with significant levels of complexity, and as a consequence there will be conflict: some will generate this from a sense of fear, some will be from an individual being territorial over a restricted area of interest and some will have their roots within personality. In fact, working with conflict is a key part of the leadership role. If you believe that your organisation is conflict-free, immediately go and check the school website and make sure that you have not been closed. It is useful, and one model is considered briefly here to understand our own approach to conflict – we will tend to have a signature response.

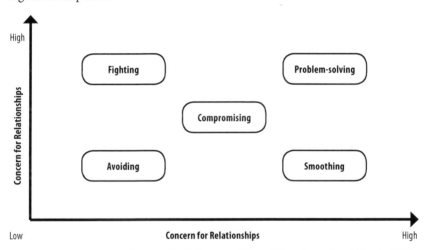

Figure 15.1 How intentions shape conflict behaviours (Adapted from Everard and Morris, 1996)

- **Avoiding.** This involves side-stepping conflict, postponing confrontation, hoping the problem will go away or pretending it does not exist. It usually imposes stress on all concerned, causes communication problems and means that decisions are made by default.

- **Fighting.** This may mean standing up for what you believe to be right or simply trying to score a personal victory. It involves bringing emotional, intellectual, hierarchical or any other form of power to bear in order to get your own way and implies a lack of respect for people's interests. It often breeds resentment, 'backstabbing' and deviousness or, if your opponent is of equal status, a 'shouting match'.

- **Compromising.** Those who compromise seek expedient, quick solutions that satisfy both parties. Focus is often less on the quality of the solution or on finding a creative solution than on finding middle ground. A compromise culture leads to wheeling and dealing that may be at the expense of principles and values.

- **Smoothing.** This approach is unassertive and co-operative. It puts the interests of others first. Over-use of this approach can cause other people to lose respect for you and your opinions, to ride roughshod over you, and discipline may become lax.

- **Problem-solving.** This involves working with the other party or parties to try to find a solution which goes as far as possible towards mutual satisfaction. It involves thoroughly exploring each other's interests and concerns and looking for creative alternative courses of action. The problem is that this takes time and energy and may be an excuse for postponing decisions that need to be taken.

Each style comes with strengths and potential consequences. Ideally, leaders should be able to draw on these as a repertoire for considered action. The reality tends to be that when we experience conflict we perform to our 'back catalogue' of behaviours. These summaries are how we may tend to behave, if all things are equal. Not surprisingly, if stress comes into the fray then our approach will change. Those with a pugilistic approach to conflict are likely to intensify that more aggressive style of behaviour, while those who place relationships at a premium have the potential to become more placatory and perhaps even sycophantic. Increasing levels of stress begin to act as a volume control, accentuating our normative behaviours.

The last word
Probably best if you do not feel that it always has to be yours.

16. NEEDY BUT NICE

Science has discovered that nature endows each healthy human conception with the wonderful array of living templates – an infinitely rich treasure house of incomplete patterns that instinctively seek completion in the environment from the moment of birth, and that continue to do so as we grow and evolve throughout our lives. These patterns are expressed as physical and emotional needs and are in a state of continuous ebb and flow ... It is precisely the way needs are met, by the impact the life has on them, that determines the individual nature, character and mental health of each person.

(Tyrrell and Griffin, 2013, p. 4)

Since childhood, I have been an inveterate reader of cereal boxes while I am eating my breakfast. Sometimes there were special offers and then there was the nutritional information. It was all there: Thiamin, Riboflavin and Niacin. Vital information such as the Reference Index gave me the percentage of these vital vitamins that were being provided by my cereal of choice. Two Weetabix biscuits would supply about a third of my daily requirement of iron. Riveting stuff, which opens up the potential criticism of a particularly bad pun. It was also gratifying to note that this cereal was endorsed by Her Majesty the Queen. When I was a science teacher, many lessons were occupied with the details of the outcomes of vitamin deficiencies: scurvy, rickets and beriberi. Just as we have nutritional needs, so too do we have emotional needs. These are less easy to specify and they cannot be individually quantified according to our body mass. Their lack, however, is just as devastating as the horrors of poor nutrition.

There have been a number of theorists who have stepped into the area of human needs. Aside from issues around mental health and wellbeing there is also the connection with motivation. These needs require satiation and exert a powerful influence on our lives as we try to meet them. Some of the seminal work has its roots as far back as the 1940s. Bowlby published widely on the effects of maternal deprivation and attachment. He sought to show how a lack of opportunity for intimacy between the mother and child could lead to significant problems in terms of behaviour and the development of social relationships (Bowlby, 1951). His work caused considerable interest and he was commissioned to write the World Health Organisation's report on this area in 1951.

A contemporary, Abraham Maslow, was also exploring the area of human needs. He published his theory in 1943. This postulated these needs as being arranged in a hierarchy, the most basic level being physiological where the needs to be warm, fed and not thirsty were seen as overriding. Ascending his hierarchy, there are requirements that we feel safe and develop a social interaction and a feeling of belonging. Finally, there is the level of self-actualisation, the point at which we engage in thinking, debate and creativity. There has been considerable criticism of Maslow's theories, with concerns being expressed about the empirical basis that underlies them (Hofstede, 1984). The persistence of Maslow's work probably comes more from the resonance that it has with human experience, rather than from the quality of the research itself. It has supported thinking that in order to undertake complex cognition we must ensure that other more subordinate needs have been sorted out first. At a practical level, you can see how this has entered the school curriculum with the development of breakfast clubs.

It is suggested that a less polemic view of human needs has been developed by Griffin and Tyrrell (2003) who suggested a list of nine essential or Primal Needs. They developed these from clinical practice rather than from empirical research. They have, however, been exposed to peer-review and retained a practical integrity that has underpinned a great deal of therapeutic practice. The following is a review of these nine Primal Needs:

1. **A sense of safety and security:** This may well mean a secure home life, employment which is not under threat, and absence of health-related issues probably living in a location where there is an absence of physical violence. The hallmark is an absence of anxiety.

2. **Giving and receiving attention:** Most people like to be listened to and in turn there is a pleasure in being selected as someone who is offered time with another. Paradoxically, there may be times when this need is held in balance and we wish to establish boundaries to limit interactions. Being ignored or dismissed does not feel like a good experience. However, you can see that these are not entirely discrete packets of need and being ignored could also impact upon our need for self-esteem and potentially erode our sense of status.

3. **Friendship:** The overwhelming majority of people require some level of connectivity with another human being and we express this as friendship, companionship, love and intimacy.

4. **Having a sense of autonomy and control:** It is unsettling if circumstances render us impotent to the point where we feel that we

cannot adequately influence events. This was very much my experience when I went skiing; however, enough of my personal problems. This is not about becoming a 'control freak', feeling that we must direct everything that is going on around us. Similarly, developing what Seligman (1975) deemed learned helplessness: behaviour that was typical of someone who has endured repeatedly painful or otherwise adverse stimuli that they are unable to find a way to escape or avoid. Seligman linked such a state with the development of depression.

5. **Belonging to a wider community:** Isolation is a very powerful sponsor of rumination. Many of these primal needs require a community context for them to be adequately met. In terms of leadership (especially where the leader is tasked to transform a failing school or academy), the role can be a lonely one. It may well not be appropriate for the leader, at that phase of development, to enter into relationships within the organisation. It strongly argued that compensatory relationships are accessed within another community.

6. **Physical needs:** Leadership is significantly cognitive, but our brains are located within a physical frame. It is erroneous to see that frame as separate and merely being a support system. Contemporary thinking recognises that there are deep connections between the body and the mind in terms of the functions both. It is imperative, therefore, that our physical needs are met and that we have an appropriate diet, exercise and sleep. Further, we need to ensure that we are not adversely affected by developing excessive reliance on stimulants and depressants, *eg* coffee or alcohol.

7. **Self-esteem:** Self-esteem is frequently talked about, but all too often misunderstood. It is a subject in its own right and is not about what we think about ourselves but very much how we feel about ourselves. Schools often have a somewhat optimistic view about their impact on students, believing that they are promoting self-esteem. This will happen in some cases but often the best-case scenario is that they do no further harm. As far as possible, it is helpful to have a realistic view of ourselves, neither viewing ourselves as better than we really are, nor, of course, undervaluing ourselves. In auditing or resetting our self-esteem, a good coach can be of considerable value.

8. **Having a sense of achievement and creativity:** Our brains are hardwired to achieve the completion of tasks. Where these are not completed, we open loops. When we complete a task our brains

reward this by delivering dopamine, a pleasurable neurotransmitter. There is a further dimension to developing a sense of achievement and this results from stretching ourselves, going that little bit further. We can gain hugely from the achievement of meaningful goals. However, there is always the requirement that we undertake some tasks which present us with a high challenge coupled with our having a relevant array of skills. This will generate a good state, what Csikszentmihalyi (1990) came to call 'flow'. Of course, the other way round is a recipe for stress and anxiety.

9. **A sense of status:** It is important to feel that we are recognised, belong and that we are valued. The word 'status' has attracted a great deal of baggage and can become synonymous with lifestyle, clothing, watches and, inevitably, cars. However, the degradation of its usage should not be allowed to mask the fact that it is a primal need. While it means different things to different people, at its heart, authentic status is about being valued – being recognised as a good parent or a valued friend may be enough. In leadership terms, it is often about being valued for what we have achieved or how we have related with other people and not for the fact that we have a designated parking slot. Where leaders understand status in an objective way, they tend to carry titles lightly and place a high value on performance. The distortions around status usually come from a misapplication to meet an individual's need for recognition.

I would suggest, that identification of Primal Needs by Griffin and Tyrrell (2003) differs significantly from the framework presented by Maslow (1943). The emphasis of the latter was strongly linked to developing a theory of human motivation and suggested the lower level of need had to be met before thinking problem-solving could be achieved successfully. Griffin and Tyrrell (2003), on the other hand, suggest that human beings have a cocktail of needs; and whereas the balance of the ingredients can vary between people, they are all required to secure wellbeing and in turn to support the delivery of outstanding performance. Rather like the vitamins that were the staple of my childhood reading, a day without one of these will not precipitate an immediate breakdown in a health, and in the same way the absence of a given primal need will not cause us to spiral into mental health problems.

However, we all have all of these primal needs and their sustained neglect or absence will have consequences. Modern life can make meeting these needs more challenging: families are breaking down and isolating individuals from their nurturing social context, social mobility imposes repeated challenges to reform networks, short-term contracts can make the sustention of status difficult to maintain. Often, the media is pernicious in the way that it projects threat and potential apocalypse and challenges our feelings of personal safety and security. I work for University College London and regularly travel from Dorset to Bloomsbury. I usually stop at the Fleet Services on the M3 to use the conveniences. I have developed a habit of not looking at the sensationalist newspaper headlines in the entrance. They reset my brain in an unhelpful way for the rest of the journey. This is not about escapism – I have concerns over many world issues – but it is about managing my thinking.

Two suggested strategies are offered for the consideration of these Primal Needs:

1. Regularly review your own needs, perhaps reflecting on those times when you have not felt good. Ask yourself the question, 'What needs have been meet and which have not?'. In the final chapter, there is a suggested review process that can be carried out on a weekly basis. If you identify particular needs which are not being met, or which are being met inadequately, then respond to the concern by drawing up an intentional action plan.

2. It is better to try and ensure that each need is met from several sources. I have come across a number of people who have recently retired. Initially, they are great advocates of this new-found freedom. Some months on and they start to struggle as their identity and status is challenged as they can no longer define it in terms of their work role. Some find good solutions and others start to posture and exaggerate their past contributions and their significance. It is always good to meet your needs across a range of contexts.

The title of this chapter is a parody of the 1970s and 1980s cream cake advertising slogan 'naughty but nice'. Astonishingly, this was the product of the creative mind of Salman Rushdie who went on to achieve fame for his controversial book *The Satanic Verses* (1986).

17. BRANDING IS NOT BELONGING

To be rooted is perhaps the most important and least recognised need of the human soul. Uprootedness is by far the most dangerous malady to which human societies are exposed.

(Simone Weil)

When you go into a store that has a national presence, have you noticed that it is immediately recognisable? My daughter-in-law worked as a visual merchandiser for the John Lewis partnership and explained how committed they are to their 'brand'. Many shops also share that phenomenon; some issue a loyalty card in order to reinforce that sense of belonging. A moment's reflection will suggest that however pleasant and identifiable the retail experience is, it is only for a moment. We may well be enthusiasts for a particular brand but we certainly do not belong. Branding is not belonging.

The changes in English education at the current time are extensive, untried and possibly questionable. There has been a very rapid shift towards neoliberalism. The outcome of this policy has been a significant erosion of the role of local authorities and the increasing aggregation of schools into groupings of various sizes. Many of these come under the heading of multi-academy trusts (MATs). Recent research (Male *et al*, 2017) suggests that there are almost as many stories about their formation as there are MATs themselves. For this research, I carried out a series of interviews with the CEOs of some of these MATs. For some of these new-style leaders, a new golden age dawned, while others were arranging their schools like some kind of educational laager, circling the wagons to protect against imminent threat.

Many of these groupings are drawn together from disparate schools. Some of the groups spanned large geographic areas, others had drawn together CEVA schools with existing maintained schools. What was common was a desire to establish some identifiable quality with their particular schools. Frequently, significant work was being undertaken to develop their 'brand'. In some cases, there was a common uniform, with the trust's logo taking precedence over that of the individual school. Behind the scenes, there was a unifying tsunami of policy, protocol and procedure. Unsurprisingly, in borrowing ideas from the corporate world, a corporate feel was being imparted.

So, does this matter? I would suggest, strongly, that it does. When we engage with a commercial corporate presence as a customer, we experience a service provision. This model is wholly inadequate to underpin the development of education in our schools. The latter institutions are not service providers *per se*. Even the most cursory exploration of psychology – such as the venerable Maslow or the more contemporary Primal Needs approach – suggests that members of the schools will have essential needs that must be met before they engage with higher-order thinking. These include the need to be listened to, to be given some level of significance, sense of control and a feeling of belonging. Such foundational needs are unlikely to be met by engaging with the world of corporate feel education.

In many cases, our clients (the pupils and students) remain with us for extended periods of time – *eg* seven years in secondary education. If there is anything self-evident, the period of schooling embraces a crucial time of personal formation. The primary-aged child engages with others in a process of socialisation; the adolescent goes into neural meltdown and then explores their own self-identity. There is a need to provide a safe and engaged developmental community. Such a community needs a hallmark of acceptance and have within it wise, caring adults who have the individual interests of the children at heart.

The antidote to juvenile corporate alignment can be found through place and belonging. A strong leader who understands not only reductionist pupil achievement, but sees their role in promoting social, emotional competence, allied to generating an environment of wellbeing, will find 'place and belonging' a powerful paradigm through which to understand what they are doing and from which to interpret the culture that they have to develop in order to produce a sustainable learning community.

Few leaders have the chance to work on a blank canvas and create a new organisation. Most of us, whether at faculty, department, phase or whole school/academy level, have to rework or even overpaint an existing canvas. This was very much the focus of Chapter 2, where the underlying picture was incredibly persistent. As a leader, we articulate our focus, the strategic direction that we intend to travel. In doing so, we consciously or carelessly create organisational culture. Sometimes, a preoccupation with pressing agendas such as raising pupil achievement can mean that we give scant attention to the cultural wake that we are creating. Schein would argue that having a proficiency in creating and regulating culture is not a leadership nicety but a core role:

The only thing of real importance that leaders do is to create and manage culture. If you do not manage culture, it manages you, and you may not even be aware of the extent to which this is happening.

(2004, p. 11)

As a leader exercises agency, there will be a cumulative effect. Even a fragmented and poorly thought-through strategy will coalesce and generate a culture. One of the outcomes of the leader's agency (or indeed its lack) will be the emergence of an organisation within which people feel rooted, or, conversely, one in which they feel alienated. This was very much the line of research around place and belonging initiated by Riley (2013 and 2017). The research team applied the prism of place and belonging to a number of situations and found that the results were remarkable in terms of pedagogy, inclusion and wellbeing. As part of the research team myself, one situation still stands out in my mind. We were working with a school in south London shortly after the murder of Fusilier Lee Rigby, in 2013. One of the men eventually convicted for the murder was an ex-student of this school and another ex-student was the person who cradled the dying soldier in her arms. The school wanted to find ways in which children joining the school (particularly as a result of people movement) might connect with the positive culture of the school and not seek their identity with less constructive groups. This generated a great deal of creative thinking around place and belonging and the school was rewarded with notable success.

At the time of writing, the Great Yarmouth Charter Academy has been making the news amidst allegations of having a draconian approach to pupil discipline. Adams, writing in *The Guardian*, records the academy's advice to teachers on how to deal with pupils who feel sick:

We all know children say things like that to get out of work. You never pretend to be ill to get out of work because we expect you to work through it. If you feel sick we will give you a bucket. If you vomit – no problem! You've got your bucket. That's probably all your body wanted – to vomit. If you are really ill we will make sure you get all the attention you need.

(Adams, 2017)

Their zero-tolerance approach to discipline will subdue most but stands as a polar opposite of the meaning of education, which is usually understood as a process whereby learning is facilitated. It is unlikely to develop autonomous learners or be the pathway to fostering a compassionate society. There will be a cultural wake that is about short-term, limited objectives that seem to have become disconnected from with the long game.

Contrast this with a vignette taken from Riley *et al* (2017, p. 21):

Hampton Court House: An 'all through' independent school with 240 pupils, occupying an 18th-century Manor House adjoining Bushy Park.

Headteacher Guy Holloway has a background in film production, acting, music, journalism and education. He 'grew' Hampton Court House and was always likely to produce a 'school' less ordinary, making the decision not to call Hampton House a school, he says. He's very clear that Hampton Court House needs to be a 'place' where things happen.

As you enter Hampton Court House, the central atrium is dominated by sofas and easy chairs occupied by adolescents spread-eagled in the way that only they are so good at. What are they doing? Closer inspection reveals that these youngsters are engrossed in their work; completing and extending work and revising for their forthcoming examinations. Hampton Court House is famed for its advocacy of a later start to the day for sixth formers. The circadian rhythms of adolescents, Guy tells us, run on a different time frame and high-quality learning needs to accommodate this.

Reflecting on the 'prism of place and belonging', there is little doubt that the central atrium is the beating heart of the school. Daily Assemblies are held here. The *space* reverberates with the sound of lunch-time recitals and *ad hoc* musical 'happenings'. It's the *space* where people and ideas converge.

Hampton Court House seeks to place people at the centre of everything it does. Young people are encouraged to be themselves. There's recognition that staff have lives too. Staff get pregnant and so child care provision has been developed to support them as parents. It is not uncommon to see sixth formers walking alongside toddlers, or staff speaking to pupils whilst holding their own child.

On the surface, it might seem that the leadership has torn up the educational rule book. Beneath the surface, there is a real sense that they have rediscovered it. The emphasis on achieving fluency in other languages and developing a strong appreciation of the aesthetic opens new horizons for young people. The determination to use the external spaces and vistas which surround the school generates a sense of connectedness. It's all about the young people: values of respect and tolerance.

'The best thing about this school,' a young person told us, 'is that it's not like a school at all.' The children and young people at Hampton Court House clearly feel that they belong in this educational home from home.
(Reproduced with kind permission of the authors)

Much of the above is about children, but it also holds true for adults working in organisations. I receive referrals from local GPs. It is suggested that many of the problems around recruitment and retention – and also with the referrals made to me by GPs – are a consequence of stress. This is a testimony to the dysfunctionality of leadership practice in some schools and academies. However, much of the focus of this book is about leaders and leadership. In many ways, leaders are even more vulnerable as they are positioned both within the organisation and, in some ways, on the outside as well. They can find that achieving a sense of belonging is challenging, and yet, like all human beings, they too have a deep-seated need to be anchored in a sense of belonging.

Psychologists have argued that all of us have needs and this was explored in the previous chapter, 'Needy but Nice'. Maslow (1943) presented his 'hierarchy' of such needs. His argument was that our requirement to feel fed, dry, safe and included will take precedence over our engagement with higher-order cognitive activity. Some 60 years later, Griffin and Tyrrell (2003) took this further by cataloguing 11 primal needs. These include the following:

- Routinely feeling safe

- Being able to give and receive attention.

- Having a sense of some control and in influence over events in life

- Having a feeling of belonging to a wider community

- Having a sense of status and a reasonably defined role in life

- Having a sense of meaning and purpose

Each element of this selection will be met, in part at least, as we have a sense of belonging within an organisation. If we do not feel that we belong, we will experience a sense of alienation and are likely to dissociate from the school's aims, and our wellbeing will be adversely affected.

One writer in the field, Seligman (2008), has developed the PERMA model to suggest routes to happiness (Figure 17.0). This again places a stress on engagement or connection with others, and in turn strongly parallels the idea of place and belonging.

In brief, Seligman's research-based model suggests that positive experiences or emotions are of value but that their impact is transient. So, though your emotions might be stirred at a great concert or looking at a beautiful view the feelings will be a bit of a Chinese meal: satisfying in the short term; but rather soon, the hunger returns. Such wellbeing is often termed 'hedonistic'. Seligman

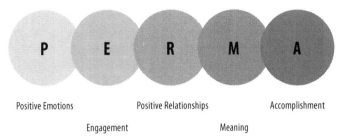

Figure 17.0: Introducing a new theory of wellbeing (Seligman, 2008)

argues that it is richer experiences such as being embedded in a network of nurturing relationships and identifying with a purpose greater than oneself that are found to be of more profound significance. These lead to 'eudaimonic' or 'fulfilment-based wellbeing'. Not only is the latter richer, but without it being enacted the hedonistic experiences have little impact or substance.

This model suggests that developing the concept of place and belonging has a self-evident impact. As belonging is addressed, networks of positive relationships develop. In turn, as a sense of belonging grows there is a connection with the idea of identifying with a wider purpose, leading to eudaimonia. As a 'starter for ten', simply feeling that you are a part of an organisation and identifying with its activities and aspirations will do nicely.

Take three schools

John (not his real name), a very experienced school leader, moved through a succession of senior posts in international schools. This was not a 'hit-and-run' approach but a considered and planned progression with each school benefiting from his leadership in turn. All of these schools were at different places in terms of their development, and also each was set in very different cultural contexts. So, in turn:

School 1: Following success in his first headship, John moved to a larger school for a second headship, taking charge of an established junior school in a mixed phase campus in Asia. This involved working with an executive head as a line manager and alongside other headteachers on the same campus. The school covered KS2 and had some 800 pupils. The role of the individual school headteacher was, in essence, being the steward of extant norms and values.

This experience of headship was in a country with a significant ex-pat community. John had young children (7 and 9) and these provided connections with other families. He was also a member of a church and played in a rock band. So, there were a number of social interfaces.

School 2: This was a very different sort of headship. A group in the Netherlands were planning a further international junior school and John was appointed as headteacher. The post was established a year in advance of this school opening and he was tasked with creating a distinctive organisation within the overall framework of the group. On opening, he had a mix of new staff and some reluctant transferees from other schools within the group.

John's strategy included drawing the staff together. He decided to undertake three activities: one where they were all on a level, one that would be universally disliked and one that would be universally seen as positive. The 'leveller' was developing the use of interactive white boards, a skill where they had no resident experts. The 'disliked' activity was an electronic based assessment process – 'after all, nobody likes assessment, and if they are disliking something that is unavoidable then they would not be disliking him'. The 'positive' was to initiate marking in green, a friendlier colour than the usual searing red. However, this well-received approach to marking had an unexpected consequence. One day, a member of staff came to see him in an angry mood and asked for a green pen. John was not quite sure what he wanted. He managed to find a green biro but this offer was rejected. Eventually, it became clear that the staff usually referred to issues that needed a decision as 'requiring a green pen', and it was actually a decision that the member of staff wanted. They had apparently created a distinctive culture in line with Basil Bernstein's group-defining restricted code. This was utilised by the SLT and new staff were even presented with a fountain pen filled with green ink and sent away to find its meaning. Within three years, they had created a culture where they 'belonged to each other' and were 'in it together'.

Meanwhile, John was heavily involved with a local church, playing music and, rather uniquely for an English national, he had formed a cycle club in the Netherlands. His wife made friends through undertaking an intensive Dutch language course. Their daughters, now 12 and 14, were also a source of social connection. The subsequent move to another school was to be a significant fracture from this established lifestyle.

School 3: This was again in Asia where he headed up a school that had grown to around 1000 pupils in a ten-year period. John was welcomed and found leading the school demanding in terms of time but thoroughly fascinating. Regrettably, this headship did not work out and he returned to the UK sooner than he originally intended.

The issues of leading schools are complex and this vignette cannot capture every dimension of what happened. However, what did emerge was that John found himself more isolated than he had been in the Netherlands. They had gone to the Asian school leaving their (now grown-up) daughters back in the UK. He also found that the indigenous culture was less accessible. He and his wife lived some 30 minutes' drive from the school and they lived in a very pleasant location amongst ex-pats and affluent nationals. However, they found their social interactions much reduced.

Undoubtedly, John was experiencing some level of grief as a result of leaving a rich and connected lifestyle in the Netherlands. Whilst his arguably premature move back to the UK cannot be explained exclusively in terms of feelings around belonging, his sense of relative isolation inevitably contributed to his decision. Speirs (2016) concludes that working in an international school can be challenging because the school community has a high turnover rate of staff, making the development of relationships difficult. They also noted that support for senior staff was often limited, especially as they were likely to be confronted by complex issues derived from staff turnover and cultural engagement.

Badge engineering

Badge engineering is less popular with manufacturers than it was some years ago. Many prefer a distinct brand identity to lookalikes that differ only in terms of minor details, a badge and the price. For example, many components are shared across the Volkswagen group, *eg* Skoda, SEAT and even some Audis. The movement to MATs has resulted in aggregations of disparate schools and in some cases the imposition of a corporate branding approach; perhaps a common uniform colour or logo seems to echo this somewhat shallow engineering practice. In some instances, MATs have adopted an approach that seeks to create a common reception area, with some going as far as banishing children's work from such hallowed portals. Only the MATs insignia and approved publicity photos are allowed. In all probability, this is unlikely to create that much-sought-after identity.

The essential identity of a school/academy lies with its values, relationships, and narrative. For staff, the four pillars of trust – communication, leadership competency, compassion and consistency – will reinforce that sense of belonging.

For the heads/principals there is an inherent isolation in such a role. They are gatekeepers to employment and promotion, they monitor performance and they are also the repository of confidential information that they cannot share widely, if at all. If belonging is germane to resilience, wellbeing and ultimately to sustaining leadership performance, then a context for belonging needs to be found not as an occasional distraction but as a central task. John met this primal need through music and even cycling. An isolated leader is a very vulnerable leader. Flintham again:

If I'd had sustainability strategies I'd have seen a way forward. The only one I had was more of the same: I enjoyed innovating which gave me satisfaction but ironically caused me to work even longer hours. I had no one professionally to turn to. I would have liked a professional listening partner (to share it all with) but (internal staff) problems meant that sort of relationship couldn't work at school and I suffered from the professional loneliness and isolation. My self-belief was undermined. I felt a good head would have solved this, and I had no one to convince me otherwise.

(2003b, p. 7)

18. THE DEATH OF COACHING

> Coaching, for a number of reasons, is a fundamental component of any movement towards personalizing learning. First, it embodies in a one to one relationship, many of the most important principles of personalizing learning in that it focuses on the individual learner. Second, it is a proven strategy in moving individuals towards learning for understanding – it is probably one of the most effective and personal learning and teaching strategies.
>
> (West-Burnham and Coates, 2005, p. 85)

There is something of the racehorse about the senior leader's ability to perform at a high level but there is often an air of fragility. Like most analogies, however, if extended too far it begins to break down. On the one hand, the racehorse performs intermittently whilst the leader exhibits high performance routinely. The race-ready horse is the output of a sophisticated training regime overseen by a trainer. Outstanding racehorse trainers facilitate and secure outstanding results. Would it not be reasonable to expect that, in a similar way, a school/academy-ready leader or a middle leader would also be supported? In the latter case, this would be a coach and not a trainer.

In 2003, the Labour Government launched The London Challenge. This was intended to run until 2008 but was extended until 2011. It was very much an intensive care project intervention and is credited with initiating significant improvement in London Schools, especially in five specifically nominated London Boroughs.

The London Challenge was supported by an extensive range of professional development programmes, one of which was mentor and coach training. I was one of these trainers and saw hundreds of consultants and senior leaders trained as mentors/coaches. Early in the delivery of this highly scripted programme were the stories of the origins of the terms mentor and coach, the former being traced back to Homer's *Odyssey* and the role of an ineffectual elderly guardian who failed to support Odysseus's son. The concept of a coach takes us back to the evolution of horse-drawn transport in medieval Europe.

I was not convinced that these stories captured the essence of what we were trying to achieve. More particularly, the programme failed to connect with the more contemporary origins of this highly effective process. In its modern incarnation, the work of Timothy Gallwey (1974) is seminal. O'Connor and Lages (2007) describe the publication of Gallwey's *The Inner Game of Tennis* as being 'the tipping point for the start of coaching as we know it today' (p. 23).

Gallwey graduated in English Literature from Harvard, but it was tennis that gripped his imagination and he became a tennis coach. He worked in the 1970s at the sports centre that was part of the Esalen Institute near San Francisco. Esalen was a key centre for the development of humanistic psychology. It brought together a number of luminaries such as; B F Skinner, Aldous Huxley, Abraham Maslow, Fritz Perls, Virginia Satir and Carl Rogers. At times, Esalen was teetering on the brink of becoming very 'alternative'; however, it was certainly a hotbed for new thinking about human potential and its development.

A significant part of the work at Esalen was the development of their EST programme in 1971. EST (the Latin for 'it is') was a self-awareness programme that used a one-to-one coaching approach. In a ten-year period, over one million people attended this. A 'spin off' from the programme was the development of the 'Design Your Life' courses in 1988 by Thomas Leonard. It was really from his work and that of his acolyte Laura Whitman that coaching was to develop in the 1990s, in America.

Backtracking to Gallwey. He distilled this emergent thinking from Esalen in his book *The Inner Game of Tennis* (1974). Starting with tennis, he argued that when a player goes on court he faces two opponents. One is the physical opponent: the other competitor on the other side of the net. The other opponent is within and is more challenging to deal with. This inner opponent may well perceive the game as being a threatening situation; limiting beliefs with origins as far back as childhood may intrude. Often, this will manifest in the player's self-talk as phrases such as 'The other player is looking on form and they beat X last week', or 'I am really playing out of my league here'.

Staying with tennis, though other sports are available, it is now unremarkable for commentators discussing a top player, like Andy Murray, to talk about mental state or his psychological preparedness or the impact of his marriage or the birth of his child on his performance. This is very much the legacy of Gallwey's thinking and advocacy. Similarly, top sports performers will employ coaches to help them secure not only peak physical fitness but also to develop and maintain a winning mind-set.

In 1970, Sir John Whitmore, the former racing driver, also studied at Esalen. He returned to the UK and became pivotal in developing business coaching in the UK, though his reach remained international. Whitmore is perhaps most famous for the development of the GROW coaching model (1992). As an aside, he was also arrested in Florida for riding on the roof of a car driven by his friend Steve McQueen, while only wearing his underpants.

This is very much a thumbnail sketch of the origins of contemporary coaching and its links to the human potential movement. This genealogy makes it all the more surprising that so much of the coaching in the educational world is dominated by deploying a problem-solving, cognitive-based model. Many coaches that I have encountered have subverted the GROW model and use it to provoke their clients to select solutions to problems with scant attention being given to their emotional or psychological state.

Perhaps the title of the chapter is a little overblown and may seem like an attempt at paraphrasing Mark Twain's (partly apocryphal) quip that the reports of his death had been somewhat exaggerated. However, in the last 15 years I have trained some 2000 coaches, mainly in the UK but also in Qatar, Colombia, China, Netherlands and the Republic of Ireland. Most have improved their communication skills, perhaps 80% have developed the skills to support someone thinking issues through (a pragmatic approach) and probably between 5% and 10% have really understood this wider frame of performance coaching. I have witnessed this latter group progressively develop their skills to support leadership 'tune up' and to do so with skills that transcend capacity building with compassion.

Coaching or mentoring?

In the early delivery of coach training in the UK there was a convoluted interest in the difference between coaching and mentoring. The writers of the programme used by the London Challenge used the term 'mentoring-coaching' to try and solve the problem of this conundrum (Pask and Joy 2007). Scattered through the literature on coaching and mentoring are a plethora of definitions and this is not helped by the fact that many of these contradict each other.

Two seminal writers on the subject, Megginson and Clutterbuck (2012, p. 6), argue for a difference between the two and then appear to cloud the issue by considering terms such as 'helpee' or 'helped'. An undisclosed member of the writing partnership likes the term 'player' and even 'learner' is considered. They do acknowledge the overlap of the two processes. This range of terminology does not really help in resolving the confusion that is often expressed around this issue.

Rogers brings a note of common sense to the debate:

> In practice, mentoring does have overtones of implying that the older and
> wiser person will be passing on their advice. Where this is so, mentoring
> is a different activity from coaching. Where coaching principles apply,
> mentoring and coaching are synonyms for the same process. In practice,
> mentoring is coming to seem like an older fashioned word for coaching.
>
> (2012, p. 17)

Probably the difference lies more with the angst of the coach than with
practicalities of execution.

Dimensions of coaching

Much of education is locked in a limiting, knowledge transmission model: those
that know share with those who as yet are unenlightened:

> Views that we should be establishing traditional, transmissive teaching
> methods more strongly are challenged, as predominately adult-led
> instruction does not help students develop and articulate ideas for
> acquiring higher-level thinking, or integrate helpful values and attitudes
> for independent minds.
>
> (Sage, 2017, p.5)

With so much of education locked in this mind-set, it is not surprising that
this has gone viral within coaching. Much professional practice is wedded
to a deductive model of thinking. We amass knowledge and then apply this
to specific problems and issues. Consider, for a moment, going to the doctor
with concerns about chronic knee pain. The expectation is that years of study
and experience will be focused on your problem in order to make a diagnosis
and hopefully suggest some resolution. Inductive thinking is the opposite
way around. An individual's problem or issue is considered and learning
and potential solutions are drawn from this. The latter is at the heart of
coaching where this experience is expressed, questioned and this becomes the
springboard for learning and action. Grasping the difference between these two
is fundamental to understanding the nature of coaching and then unsheathing
its undoubted power.

At the heart of the coaching process is the establishment of rapport, which
becomes the conduit for effective dialogue. If this is not established, or if
it begins to wane, then the dialogue becomes like spraying a Teflon-coated
surface: nothing sticks. The coaching is then an amalgam of listening (which
provides the client with a reflective space) and questions (which have been

recognised since the time of Socrates as the major driver of learning). Of course, there will also be plan of action coming from the coaching; anything less would just be a chat. Coaching is rigorous and challenging. It seems deceptively simple but this apparent simplicity can mask a profound pedagogy.

Selecting a coach

Coaching was never intended to be a sort of 'roadside assistance' for leaders who have broken down. It will service such a need. However, effective coaching should support enhanced leadership performance and sustained and safe engagement with the role. There are no formal requirements for the accreditation of coaches – as, indeed, there are not for counsellors or psychotherapists.

This book will provide a number of possibilities for thinking through intentional coaching. However, you should be clear what it is that you want to gain from the coaching relationship. While additional things may emerge when you are being coached, serendipity is not a great starting place. The following are ten areas to explore with a potential coach:

- What is the model of coaching? Good coaches will be delighted to tell you how they go about coaching and the model that they use. An inadequate coach will provide a confused answer, perhaps major on their use of the GROW model or mumble about being eclectic. Such responses probably indicate that they are not the coach you are looking for.

- Ask about their approach to confidentiality. No competent coach will bridle at such an enquiry. They will certainly limit the balance of such confidentiality to exclude the illegal and safeguarding issues.

- Does the person have a coach themselves? It would seem somewhat disingenuous to be an advocate of coaching and then not avail yourself of its benefits.

- Enquire about the time commitment. Quality coaching is an intense process and generally one hour is sufficient. Most coaches are unashamedly offering their services in order to earn a living. There is nothing wrong with that. However, if there are signs that they wish to build a long-term relationship then this could indicate mixed motives. In general, most specific issues are dealt with in six sessions. This does not preclude working on a separate issue at a later date or even sequentially. In the final chapter of this book, there is a different way of working with a coach to effect a review process.

- What is the cost for the coaching and is it inclusive of the coach's travel expenses? Also, ask if it is possible to terminate the coaching contract if either party feels that the coaching relationship is not beneficial. If you, as client, were to do so, is there a financial penalty?

- Does the coach have a supervisor? This is another coach with whom they regularly discuss their work and any issues that have surfaced within themselves. Consider an ex-headteacher-turned-coach who faced particular problems in their own work and where a parallel situation in the coaching has caused past events to resurface. It is more common for counsellors to work in this way. While the absence of a supervisor should not preclude employing the coach, the presence of one is certainly evidence of the person working in a professional way.

- Ask the coach if they are a member of a professional organisation. Such membership is not mandatory, but certainly if they are a member of an organisation such as the European Mentoring and Coaching Council (EMCC) or the International Coach Federation (UK), this could be taken as being a positive. You might also ask about how they trained as a coach and how they are currently securing their continuing professional development.

- Enquire how they respond to issues of wellbeing and mental health. They should certainly have strategies to deal with stress and anxiety and should also be clear where their boundaries lie with regard to mental health issues. As a coach, I routinely work with clients who are stressed but I would be unwilling to work with someone who was receiving treatment from a psychiatrist or a clinical psychologist.

- Certainly ask for references or testimonials. This can sometimes be a problem as some clients are reticent about revealing or even potentially revealing the problems that they have had to deal with. Most coaches will have clients who are willing to provide a testimonial but they may wish to do so anonymously. There is clearly a judgement to be made here.

- The final area of exploration probably requires a degree of subtlety and this is around the perception that the coach has of their role as an educator. A good coach seeks to provide strategies and tools for the client to use in the future. The aim of good coaching is to support the development of professional and personal autonomy. A poor coach will tend to build dependency and this is often evidenced by their promotion of an open-ended coaching relationship. Every coaching session should be a learning experience for the coach as well. However, the coaching relationship should not be used as a forum for the coach to get their own needs met. One coach that I was talking with had been coaching a headteacher. They then moved to becoming an *ex officio* member of the school's senior leadership team. This is, arguably, too often, too long and too far. It all came to an end when the coach arrived at the school to see the head, the coach's client, being taken to hospital in an ambulance after suffering a cardiac arrest. Just a suggestion, but the coach may just have gone a little light on the wellbeing agenda.

Coaching is a powerful support both in leadership terms and also personally. Further, high quality is not cheap; though, having said that, sometimes the inadequate charge more than they merit. It is always good policy to meet a prospective coach and interview them thoroughly. A good coach will not object, and a poor coach – well, they will probably appear more and more bewildered as the interview progresses. The objective questions will certainly guide your decision, but also pay attention to your intuition.

If something does not feel right, then that is probably the case.

19. REBOOT

Mindfulness isn't difficult. We just need to remember to do it.

(Salzberg, 2010, p. 17)

The train stopped at Clapham Junction. In itself, that was not a problem; it was the fact that that was all it did. Soon, an announcement was made that the train was delayed by a technical fault and that they were working to solve it as quickly as possible. From where I was sat, I could see a computer monitor, and I watched with fascination as they switched it off and then on. It seemed to work, as we were soon moving again. The event generated a mixed response. On the one hand, I felt some satisfaction that they had used my method of choice when dealing with IT problems. However, I also felt some disquiet that this multimillion piece of technology was being sorted using the same low-tech approach. It set me wondering: could we use the same approach with our brains? I came to the conclusion that employing a hard reset was probably not a great idea. But I was reminded that there are techniques that will reboot the brain without an intermediate phase of coma.

Three techniques are considered in this chapter: mindfulness, 7/11 breathing and the Emotional Freedom Technique (EFT). The former is a maintenance tool and the latter two are successful intervention strategies that can be used when we are stressed or dealing with invasive mind-sets.

Mindfulness

Mindfulness, with its origins in Buddhism, was seen as being somewhat alternative. It has now moved centre stage and is being widely advocated. The following quotation is from the NHS Choices website:

> Mindfulness is recommended by the National Institute for Health and Care Excellence (NICE) as a way to prevent depression in people who have had three or more bouts of depression in the past.
>
> (NHS, 2017)

There are a growing number of studies that support its use, such as Branstrom *et al* (2011) and Baer *et al* (2008).

Mindfulness is often presented in a deficit frame and is, frequently, advocated as a solution for depression and anxiety. This is not surprising when we

154

are facing such a tsunami of mental health issues. At the time of writing, a *Telegraph* (2017) article reported that one in three 'sick notes' issued by GPs is provided for mental health issues. The article also records these two responses:

> The Royal College of Psychiatrists said the figures were 'alarming', urging employers to do more to help support staff struggling with common mental health problems such as depression.

> The head of the NHS said mental health was now 'front and centre' of the health service agenda.

It is the argument of this book that it is as important, if not more important, to develop strategies to avoid these distressing and often dark conditions. This is especially true for mindfulness. Its regular use will help secure not only positive mental health but also underpin effective leadership. That cliché, 'If it ain't broke, don't fix it', may apply to your lawnmower but it definitely does not apply to your head.

Human beings are almost certainly unique in the animal kingdom in that they can reflect or even ruminate on the past and also speculate on what might happen in the future. Poor mental health and even poor performance can often be traced to spending too much time in these spaces where we have little or no agency. The more the pressure mounts, the more we try to explain how we have got into this particular position and then make predictions about the future which are quite likely to move to the apocalyptic end of the prophetic spectrum. Mindfulness is about returning us to the present and using techniques to drag us away from rumination and unlikely futures. Imagine that you are driving a car up a long and very steep gradient and the engine starts to overheat. The best strategy is to pull off the road, put the car into neutral and let it idle until it cools own.

Mindfulness does much more than let the overheated leader return to an appropriate operating temperature: it also changes the way in which they will view the very situations that they are dealing with. It objectivises the leadership in-tray. Regular engagement with mindfulness gives us this changed perspective as an enduring legacy.

The information on mindfulness is legion: web-based courses, phone apps, books, face-to-face courses and personal training. My suggestion is that you start both simply and with a commitment to incorporating it in your daily routine. Begin with as little as five minutes in the morning and then perhaps build up to two sessions each day and perhaps eventually extend these sessions to 20 minutes. I also incorporate mindfulness into other daily activities such as eating (where I slow down and savour each mouthful) and walking the dog (where I take notice of my surroundings, from the macro to the micro). I even drink tea mindfully!

Faced with this level of time commitment, many stressed and pressured leaders will dismiss the idea as great in principle but unconnected to the time demands that they are under. The simple response is that no high performer neglects effective preparation. 'Just Do It' is seldom the leadership platform of choice.

Meditation lies at the core of mindfulness and the following exercise is a great place to start and will certainly pay tangible dividends. It works best in a quiet place where you will not be disturbed. You will need an upright but comfortable chair.

Stage 1 (60 Seconds)

Breathe purposefully

Sit in the chair in an upright position with the small of your back pressed against the back of the chair. With your feet flat on the floor, place your hands in a comfortable position on your thighs. Close your eyes or let them look forward in an unfocused way. For a moment, just notice how your feet feel on the floor; it might be hard or soft. Begin to breathe purposefully, either through the nose or the mouth. Consciously breathe in and then exhale more slowly. (See the later section on 7/11 Breathing) Keep going for approximately one minute.

Stage 2 (60 Seconds)

Move at your own pace

Now, stop counting and let your breathing settle into a pace that feels natural to you. Pay attention to what each breath feels like; compare your rhythm of breathing with how you normally breathe. Observe how the breaths are formed as they start with the abdomen and then move upwards to the shoulders.

Stage 3 (60 Seconds)

Retain your focus

Continue to be aware of your breathing and this natural cadence that you have adopted. Usually, at this stage, thoughts and ideas will start to intrude; 'to do lists', appointments, challenging issues, perhaps even problem people. Do not try to exclude them or allow them to become a dominating focus. Instead, start to visualise them as a being like a cloud floating past, observed but harmless. Visualising issues in this way will allow you to acknowledge your concerns without becoming emotionally overwhelmed by them. If a thought does not drift away, it is often helpful to make a note of it on a notepad and return to your meditation.

Stage 4 (60 Seconds)

Relax

You have been focusing on your breathing. Now, simply sit, reminding yourself that there is nothing you are required to do at this time.

Stage 5 (60 Seconds)

Gratitude

Finally, call to mind something that you are grateful for. It may be a relationship, a beautiful day, improved health or even just the chance to spend some time meditating.

Connect with your body, noticing how relaxed your muscles are, the steady rhythm of your heart. If your eyes have been closed, open them. Stand up and move forward with the rest of your day in a calm and resourceful state.

(Adapted from the 'Five-Minute Meditation', Liao, 2017)

Engaging with mindfulness is not a luxury, but an essential: it increases concentration by reducing stress; it increases our range of options when we are making decisions; and it improves engagement with people by transferring attention from ourselves to them. Luders *et al* (2012) even found that this kind of meditation changes neural structure. Their work suggests that it will increase the amount of gyrification of the brain – that is, the folding of the cortex tissue on the outside of the brain. This actually allows the brain to process information faster.

7/11 breathing

This is very much a 'break the glass in case of emergency' technique. Our breathing is on autopilot for most of the time. Probably, until you read this chapter, you had not even thought about whether you were breathing or not. Unusually for a physiological function, we can take back control and regulate our breathing rate or even hold our breath.

If you purposefully breathe out longer than you breathe in, your body will calm down. This response to slowing down your breathing rate is inevitable, it is hardwired into your nervous system; there's simply no way round it for your body. Shallow rapid breathing is very much part of the stress scenario and should be avoided. The 7/11 breathing technique simply puts some structure into how we can regulate our breathing.

If you start to feel anxious or stressed:

1. Pause.

2. Focus on your breathing.

3. Breathe in through your nose to the count of 7.

4. Breathe out slowly through your mouth to the count of 11.

In a minute or so, you will have calmed down to a surprising degree. Crucially, it is about breathing slowly and deliberately and maintaining the ratio of the times that you inhale and exhale.

Weil (2015) demonstrates a variation of this technique. He advocates breathing in to the count of 4, holding whist counting to 7 and exhaling through the mouth for the count of 8. This method seems to work particularly well for getting off to sleep.

Threat actives our fight-or-flight response and stimulates the sympathetic nervous system, getting us ready for action. The parasympathetic nervous system works in the opposite manner and moves us to a bodily state of rest or relaxation. It is the out-breaths that bring this system into play. When you are startled, you will often take a sharp intake of breath. However, after a good meal you might move your chair back from the table and sigh deeply: an out-breath. Not surprisingly, a breathing technique with longer out-breaths than in-breaths will be more effective at lowering emotional arousal and it is resonant with us achieving a naturally relaxed bodily and mental state.

Emotional Freedom Technique (EFT)

We are very accomplished pattern-matchers. This means that new experiences and understandings are compared with information and we find the best fit that we hold in our memories. The example of the impact of a previous poor interview has been given earlier in the book. However, for the sake of clarity, here is a further example. Consider that you are driving an unfamiliar car. You will notice similarities and some differences with other cars that you have driven. You draw on the similarities from your memory in order to accommodate the transition to driving the new vehicle. Many of life's experiences are also attached to significant emotions. If they are positive then there is not likely to be a problem. However, if the situation that you find yourself in links to a past stressful experience then the memory will be tagged with charged emotions. Consider confronting a difficult member of staff or attending an interview when previous experiences in these areas were unsuccessful. As your brain draws on what it believes to be relevant resources, it also collects the attendant emotions. So, the fear linked to previous confrontations is now paired with this new confrontation. The disappointment associated with a failed interview now generates detrimental anxiety even before the current interview begins.

EFT was developed by Gary Craig (~1990) and has similarities with a number of other techniques such as Thought Field Therapy (TFT) and the Havening Technique. Some relate it to acupuncture, others to the ancient Chinese philosophy of Chi. Other writers such as Bakker (2013) suggest that it has little to offer than a placebo effect.

Over the years, I have explored a whole range of approaches that are peripheral to coaching such as NLP, EFT, TFT, Cognitive Behaviour Therapy (CBT) and hypnotherapy. My purpose was to see what was out there and also to extend my own 'coaching toolkit'. Just after completing an EFT practitioner's course, a headteacher asked me to coach them. On the phone, they were somewhat evasive as to the focus of our potential work together. I arranged an appointment to discuss matters further. I was somewhat taken aback to find that the key issue was that before they took a school assembly, chaired a staff meeting or attended a governors' meeting, they were violently sick in their wastepaper basket. I will admit to being thrown, having thought that something like team development might be the focus. On the ropes, I decided to use EFT and was astonished to find that it worked. This was an act of desperation and not conviction. Subsequently, I have used it many times and have repeatedly secured positive outcomes. In discussion with Will Thomas, who is an experienced coach and who also wrote the foreword to this book, he shared with me a number of similar experiences.

What follows is very much a basic introduction to the technique but it is sufficient to secure effective outcomes. Most practitioners use scaling. You might ask, 'Where do you feel the emotion or your anxiety about a particular problem is on a scale of 1-10, with 1 low and 10 high?'. This is a very subjective assessment of the issue but is useful for making a comparison on a before or after basis.

Critically, a verbal component of the process is now created: this will be a problem statement followed by a positive affirmation. Called the 'set up', this generates a statement which is repeated in whole or in part throughout the process. The following are three that I have used with different clients, bespoke statements linked to a particular issue:

- Example 1: 'Even though I am anxious about making presentations, I completely love and accept myself.'

- Example 2: 'Even though I don't like confrontation, I completely love and accept myself.'

- Example 3: 'Even though I feel inferior to other people, I completely love and accept myself.'

Once the 'set up' phrase is familiar, it is slowly repeated over and over as the EFT process is carried out.

EFT is often known as the 'Tapping Therapy' and this is now the phase that we move to, sometimes referred to as 'the sequence'. It is good to go through the points, repeating the 'set up' phrase as you move through the different points in turn. Tap as if you mean it, using two fingers, and it is fine to use either hand. Six firm taps on each point will work.

The starting point is tapping on the **side of the hand** at the root of the little finger. This is sometimes called the 'karate chop point'. Now move on as follows:

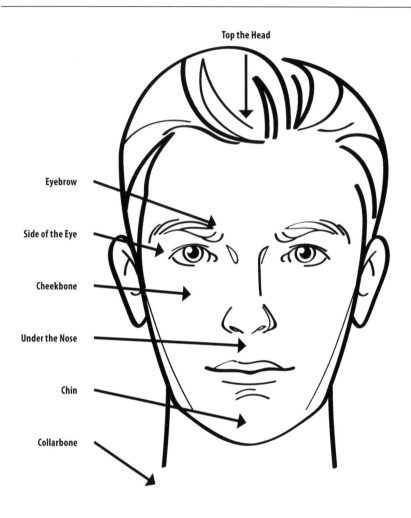

Figure 19.0 EFT Tapping Points

Top of the head: Imagine drawing a line from each ear over the top of the head and then one from your nose to the nape of your neck, then this tapping point is at the intersect.

Eyebrow: The tapping point is at the end of the eyebrow, just above the nose.

Side of the eye: This is the other end of the eyebrow on the outside corner of the eye.

Cheekbone: Drop down to a point about one inch below your pupil.

Under your nose: Tap on the concave depression above your lip. (It is actually called the philtrum.)

Chin: Here the tapping point is midway between the lower lip and the tip of the chin.

Collarbone: The actual point is where the sternum (breastbone), collarbone and first rib meet. If you move from the sternum towards the collarbone you will feel a notch. Once you have found this move left and down by two centimetres and that will take you to the point.

Underarm: You should tap a point about ten centimetres below the arm pit.

Now return to complete the cycle by tapping the 'karate chop point' whilst continuing to repeat the 'set up'.

It is suggested that you follow the order but that you remain relaxed, and if you miss a point on one cycle, then pick it up the next. Pause after three or four cycles, use scaling to assess how your issue has improved and if you need to carry on further in order to secure still further improvement. The cycle is best carried out regularly over the days that follow and repeated if there is a reoccurrence of the problem. This is the self-help version but you could wish to refine the technique with a trained practitioner.

Not everybody warms to EFT, with its origins rooted in quasi mysticism. However, my argument is that it ruptures the connection between a particular narrative and its associated emotion. There is also a recognition that change is possible, itself a powerful antidote to ensconced victimhood. It is likely that the set up phrase is a powerful positive affirmation with its present tense and first person structure. EFT seems improbable but it is a process that regularly defies expectations. It is well worth a try and has resolved some challenging situations.

Out of sight, out of mindfulness

The quotation at the opening of the chapter is from one of the pioneers in the current wave of meditation and mindfulness, Sharon Salzberg. She hits the nail squarely on the head when she argues for its routine use. Mindfulness, in particular, is being taught in schools. It is burgeoning in professional development days and classrooms. I regularly advocate its use with my clients. Often, they respond with something to the effect of 'I know all about this. We had a day on it.' Initially, I was encouraged to hear this but my optimism was soon dispelled as it became evident that their knowledge and practice were not in the same room.

These deceptively simple techniques connect with our physiology and psychological processes in profoundly beneficial ways. They must, however, be applied with a degree of persistence if they are to work. The argument has been made that anxiety and stress are either hardwired into our brains or else we have learnt negative patterns of behaviour and thinking, such as catastrophisation. Changing these is completely possible, but it is unreasonable to expect the process of change to be passive.

I am concluding with a story that certainly has its origins way back in history, though it came to my notice from *Uncommon Psychotherapy*:

> Once, a beautiful princess sat by an ornate pool in her palace grounds. As she peered down, admiring her beautiful reflection on the surface of the clear pool, her priceless crown suddenly slipped from her head and into the waters with a splash.
>
> She screamed for her attendants to retrieve her precious crown and they leapt into the waters, frantically searching, scrabbling around, a flurry of activity. But all this effort merely brought up mud and debris from the bottom of the pool, making it even harder to find the missing crown...
>
> Eventually, an old storyteller arrived on the scene. He began to tell such a riveting tale of times gone by that, despite themselves, all the princess's aides stopped searching and relaxed. Even the princess momentarily forgot about the missing crown and listened to the man's sweet words. By the time he'd finished telling his tale, not only had everyone calmed down, but the mud from the pool had settled and the waters were again clear.
>
> At that point, the storyteller reached down into the water and retrieved the princess's crown, which could now clearly be seen.
>
> (Tyrrell, 2015, pp. 45-46)

Like most metaphorical stories, it can be explored and applied in different ways. However, in this context it provides an excellent insight into the way persistent mindfulness is so relevant to the role of leadership and of decision-making in particular. The cognitive mud settles and mental clarity is secured.

20. EPITAPH OR EPIPHANY?

Am I jumping the gun, Baldrick, or are the words 'I have a cunning plan' marching with ill-deserved confidence in the direction of this conversation?

(Edmund Blackadder, *Blackadder the Third*
Curtis and Elton, 1987)

In Chapter 2, 'A Perfect Storm', Flintham's 'reservoir' papers were quoted (2003a and 2003b). These publications were originally commissioned as small-scale practitioner research for the National College for School Leadership. The original work was with a small cohort of headteachers in Nottinghamshire. Subsequently, he extended the reach of that research. For me, one of the most powerful dimensions of his conclusions was the conceptual model developed as he explored the circumstances and reasons for headteachers leaving their posts prematurely (2003b).

He concluded that these heads fell into three main categories: the striders, the strollers, and the stumblers. These were outlined in Chapter 2, but here is a brief summary:

- **Striders.** These were headteachers who could articulate their career pathway. They understood their current role as being for a limited time before they moved on. This approach created a degree of objectivity and certainly gave those in this group a sense of personal control.

- **Strollers.** This group had less-defined career plans but appeared to be professionally reflective as opposed to being ruminative. Ideally, they wanted to move on at a point where their contribution was recognised as being positive. A number chose to leave their headship to secure better work/life balances or in response to a perception that they had lost a sense of identity with the overarching framework.

- **Stumblers.** In the context of this book these are the 'at-risk' group. Their narratives frequently spoke of reaching an awareness of their predicament quite late in the day. In a number of cases, depressive illness or psychosomatic disorders had become insistent warnings that all was not well. This was the group that often alluded to the metaphor of the frog not appreciating the increasing temperature of the water until it was too late. Their departure was usually unplanned, leaving them with no positive exit strategy.

These categories are not finite and they are also not immutable. It is possible in one context to have that objective professional reflection and yet in another to become overwhelmed by events and lose essential perspective on events. What is clear is that having a process of review or audit is essential. Leaders (almost by definition) are problem-solvers and this is often sustained by having high levels of self-belief in their abilities to resolve situations. The boundary between confidence and delusion can be deceptive.

For some, this book will have been a diversion; however, without action it could serve as little more than an epitaph to a phase of leadership. Hopefully, for others the content will have be an 'epiphany', a moment of revelation when there is a realisation that leading without professional reflection and personal action is foolhardy.

Audit

Audit, review and evaluation are commonplace experiences for leaders working within organisational accountability frameworks. What follows is a person-specific process which has two aims: firstly, to ensure that individuals secure appropriate wellbeing; and secondly, to help keep our cognitive performance at a high level so that we remain creative and effective leaders.

This model operates at three levels; a weekly personal audit, a monthly narrative review and a three-monthly coaching session. This process has been developed over 15 years of working with middle and senior leaders and has been found to be very effective in identifying and initiating early intervention and also in supporting leadership efficacy. **Please note that this process should never be seen as an alternative to seeking the advice of a healthcare professional if you have concerns about your health, either physical or mental.**

The weekly personal audit

It is recommended that you complete this audit each week, preferably at a set time. You will need 30 minutes when you can reflect on your personal circumstances without interruption. It is also suggested that you undertake the audit on paper (how very Luddite, but see Chapter 14) and that you file these away and use them with a three-monthly coaching session.

There are 20 questions and each is scored using a traffic light system: red suggesting that you have significant issues in this area; amber indicating that this is an area which you are neglecting and should monitor carefully; and green is about having this particular area in hand at the present time.

Audit Area	Traffic Light Code (red, amber, green)
Daily Mindfulness (five minutes minimum)	
Quality of sleep (duration and depth)	
Use of time-management system	
Control of digital devices (possibly two fast days?)	
Handling of a specific area of conflict	
Boundaried planning time	
Listening to others	
Keeping appointments or meetings, with appropriate preparation	
Quality of diet (regularity and content)	
Consumption of alcohol	
Time with valued friends (laughter not optional)	
An action that you are proud of	
Regular exercise (at least three walks per week)	
An occasion when you have said 'no'	
Rumination or 'mental churning' around issues	
Doing something that you really enjoy	
Review your primal needs	
Expressed genuine gratitude to another person	
Brought a significant task to completion	
Spent time with those who matter to you	

Point for Action	Action (linked to Weekly Personal Audit)
1	
2	
3	

Table 20.0 Weekly Personal Audit and Action Plan

The monthly narrative review

There are two ways of doing this, both of which work well. The first is to use a digital recorder or smartphone and record, almost Radio 4 style, an account of your life over the last four weeks. This should be both personal and professional, because they are all in 'one pot'. Some people find this hard to do, so an alternative approach is to find a friend, preferably not a colleague, and just chat through the events of the preceding month. You are looking to capture between 20-30 minutes of reflective conversation.

Before undertaking this, it would be advisable to establish the conversation as being confidential. When I am coaching, I offer a guarantee of confidentiality to clients unless they share something which is illegal or where their own personal safety is a risk.

Find a quiet place to play back the recording back to yourself. Initially, you may feel slightly self-conscious but this will soon pass. As you listen to yourself, interrogate your narrative. What are the issues that are coming to the fore? Are these the issues that you expected or are they surprising? What is the general tone of your narrative? Is it positive or negative in style? Is there evidence of actions which have been inappropriately deferred? Are there specific individuals who feature prominently in your narrative? Are these individuals being discussed in positive or negative terms?

Previously, in Chapter 8, the way that a narrative becomes a filter was discussed. If we are feeling threatened by the situation that we are in, our narrative will become negative, and in turn this is linked to the way we are prioritising the information so that we give a greater prominence to the negative. The brain does this to lever behaviours which will remove us from a potentially threatening situation, and in the process it can build an increasingly toxic narrative to use as a goad to action.

It is advisable to keep these recordings. You can always archive them on a laptop or desktop. They can help track your mental and emotional trajectory over time.

The three-monthly coaching session

Mostly coaching is conducted as a block of sessions, perhaps six spread over three months. This is a very useful way to work with a coach on a specific issue. What is being suggested here is a different approach where the coach supports a regular audit of your personal and leadership journey. Not all coaches are able to undertake this. In Chapter 18, some guidance was offered in selecting a coach. Be clear about what you want from the session. It may well be that further coaching sessions will flow from the audit but it should not be seen as an inevitable or necessary outcome.

At the session, it is useful to bring your Weekly Personal Audit and your Narrative Reviews. The latter could even be sent to the coach in advance. With the coach, identify areas for development or areas for action. The coach should help you to identify slippage and to refine your action plan. I have found using a Strengths, Weaknesses, Opportunities and Threats (SWOT) analysis, working with a flipchart sized piece of paper particularly effective. I am not going to go into detail around conducting a SWOT analysis; however, they do ensure that the session does not lapse into deficit as 'Strengths' and 'Opportunities' are considered. It is very important that a negative agenda is not set. This is not a nicety but rather it takes into account the fact that the brain is set up to have an avoidance or to adopt a counter threat bias. Senge offers the following observation:

> Most adults have little sense of real vision. We have goals and objectives, but these are not visions. When asked what they want, many adults will say what they want to get rid of ... 'Negative visions' are sadly commonplace, even among very successful people. They are the by-product of a life of fitting in, of coping, of problem-solving. As a teenager in one of our programs once said, 'We shouldn't call them "grown-ups"; we should call them "given-ups"'.
>
> (1992, p. 147)

The now and the not yet

Just before the start of the First World War, if someone was asked 'What it is the most reliable form of road transport?', the answer would probably involve the horse in some way. The motor car was considered by many to be somewhat ridiculous. If you were to change the question to 'What is the likely future of road transport?', the reply would probably suggest that the future would include a much greater use of vehicles powered by internal combustion engines. However, at the time, horse-drawn carriages and carts were at their zenith. This was a point of transition, the now and the not yet. This serves as a useful metaphor for much of what is currently taking place in education. As we approach 2020, we are refining and developing what is, in essence, a Victorian/Edwardian education system. Even between 2005 and 2010, when the Building Schools for the Future initiative was taking place, there was little challenge to the basic didactic format based on units of 30 pupils.

Paradoxically, as England seeks to reform education, it has created an illusion of diversity through its fascination with neoliberalism and yet it is actually creating an educational monoculture. The intermediary layer of the Local Authority had been under threat since the 1990s as it was made to tender its services to schools which were receiving increasing shares of their 'top sliced' funding.

When Michael Gove became Secretary of State for Education in 2010, this whole process moved up several notches as he sought to drive the educational system using a neoliberalist ideology. He created a series of autonomous business units which sponsor education through groups of schools. This vision has crystallised into the establishment of MATs and this has accelerated the demise of local authority engagement with education. In the end, these MATs are service providers operating in similar ways to the way in which G4S is contracted to run prisons. Pressure is applied to the system by high-stakes testing, inspection and through regional school commissioners (RSCs). Innovation becomes restricted to meeting the demands of the contract.

Just as horse-drawn transport was at its pinnacle around 1914, so it is likely that in the future we will look at our schools and academies at the beginning of this millennium as being an anachronism. Why, in the face of significant discoveries in neuroscience, are we placing the emphasis on teaching methodology rather than developing new approaches to sponsor the acceleration of learning? Why do schools and academies remain rigidly subject-centred as burgeoning technologies configure knowledge in ever-more integrated ways? Content focus still remains paramount and we emphasise an education that is about an individualised grasp of knowledge when much of this has such a short half-life and industry demands that people work as teams.

At the conclusion of this book I would like to raise what many are seeing as a much more significant issue, that of Artificial Intelligence (AI). Sage has surveyed some – and it is just some – of the changes that are imminent:

> Oxford and Yale Universities (Grace *et al*, 2017) took the views of world AI researchers, finding that they all predicted that *every* human job will be automated within the next 120 years. However, the survey focused on the cognitive aspects of well-defined activities, but emotional ones go beyond this to question whether AI will surpass humans at being art and film critics! *The Oxford University Martin Programme on Technology & Employment* (Frey & Osbourne, 2013) suggests that half of present jobs will be fully automated within 20 years. The report by Reform (Hitchcock, 2016), a public think-tank, suggests that 90% of Whitehall's 137,000 Civil servants will be replaced by AI chatbots by 2020, saving £2.6 billion annually. Public sector workers will be affected, with 90,000 NHS administrators and 30% of doctors and nurses having duties taken over by smart machines. Jobs for middle classes, such as banking and insurance, will also be automated, but new computer simulations could rejuvenate economic planning.

Dispensing with routines allows people to focus on ideas, innovation and suggest higher-value work, but interpersonal communication (*resulting in advanced thinking*) is needed for this to occur. Greater value and attention is required for this, with 50 years of research showing that *specific* communication training and support is vital for optimum performances, giving opportunities to gain a broad skill-range (Sage, 2000). Why are we ignoring such messages and narrowing opportunities for students once they leave education?

(2017, p. 10)

The strange case of Jill Watson

At the time of writing, The Georgia Institute of Technology runs an online master's degree in computer science. The lead on the programme, Professor Ashok Goel (2014), utilises a team of eight teaching assistants (TAs) to handle some 10,000 posts and messages per course.

With a specialism in AI, Goel decided to introduce a ninth teaching assistant, Jill Watson. The latter is in fact a virtual TA based on IBM's Watson platform. There were initial 'teething' problems around the ambiguity of language and the answers had to be checked and fronted by the human members of the team. However, current developments have taken Jill's answers to 97% accuracy, though the system tends to direct the more routine questions to 'her'.

The students were not told that there was an AI-based respondent in the support team. When this was revealed, there was a uniformly positive response to the development. In fact, numbers of the students failed to identify 'Jill' correctly. Perhaps more disturbingly, some students identified some of the human TAs as the potential AI teaching assistant.

The future, it would appear, is already with us.

Called to soar

There is huge pressure on the chief executive officers of MATs and other school and academy leaders to achieve financial and educational targets. I would suggest that this is creating a new managerialism amongst those tasked with this role. In the light of the radical changes society is facing, this is the time to harness leadership creativity and not task creative individuals to rearrange the deckchairs on the *Titanic*. We cannot afford to fetter creative educationalists to support outdated systems of education that were created for a different dispensation. If only half of what has been said in the foregoing about AI moves from improbability to actuality, then education will require much more than a Govian makeover. The Vice-Chancellor of The University of Buckingham, Sir Anthony Seldon, believes that intelligent machines will replace teachers within ten years. In an interview given to *The Independent*, he went on to say:

> In the AI classrooms, each child will progress at his or her own pace. There would be no more set courses applicable to all students as teaching, carried out by emotionally sensitive machines, would be highly personalised.

(Von Radowitz, 2017)

Asked in the same interview if he was suggesting machines would replace the inspirational role of teachers, he said: 'I'm desperately sad about this but I'm afraid I am'.

Seldon's view is at the more utopian end of the spectrum. Others such as Elon Musk take a more dystopian view:

> I think we should be very careful about artificial intelligence. If I had to guess at what our biggest existential threat is, it's probably that. So, we need to be very careful. I'm increasingly inclined to think that there should be some regulatory oversight, maybe at the national and international level, just to make sure that we don't do something very foolish.

(Musk, quoted in Gibbs, 2014)

Perhaps what is surprising is that within educational community there is so little discussion about AI. If the prophecies are remotely correct then we run the danger of robots teaching children the skills to equip them for very jobs that have, actually, been replaced by robots. Education seeks to provide equality of access and opportunity and yet it is likely that perhaps 80% of children will be displaced from employment with those who have underachieved or who have been ill-served being the least equipped for a lifetime of leisure. We are entering a phase of education where mind-enabled thinkers/leaders need to take centre stage again and design education that is responsive to context.

The call must be to soar. That is the role and the right of leadership

BIBLIOGRAPHY

Adams, R. (2017) 'Norfolk school drops advice to offer pupils vomit bucket in class', *The Guardian*, 12th September. Available at: www.theguardian.com/education/2017/sep/12/norfolk-school-drops-advice-to-offer-pupils-vomit-bucket-in-class (Accessed 12th September 2017).

Allcott, G. (2016) *How to be productivity ninja*. London: Icon Books.

Allen, D. (2001) *Getting things done*. London: Piatkus.

Altricher, H. and Kemethofer, D. (2015) 'Does accountability pressure through school inspections promote school improvement?', *School Effectiveness and School Improvement* 26 (1) pp. 32-56.

American Academy of Pediatrics (2014) 'School start times for adolescents', *Pediatrics* 134 (3) pp. 642-649.

Ashley, M. (2012) 'Repairing the injured brain: why proper rehabilitation is essential to recovering function', *Cerebrum*. Available at: dana.org/Cerebrum/2012/Repairing_the_Injured_Brain__Why_Proper_Rehabilitation_Is_Essential_to_Recovering_Function/ (Accessed 1st December 2016).

Baer, R. A., Smith, G. T., Lykins, E., Button, D., Krietemeyer, J., Sauer, S., Walsh, E., Duggan, D. and Williams, J. M. (2008) 'Construct validity of the five-facet mindfulness questionnaire in meditating and nonmeditating samples', *Assessment* 15 (3) pp. 329-342.

Bakker, G. M. (2013) 'The current status of energy psychology: extraordinary claims with less than ordinary evidence', *Clinical Psychologist* 17 (3) pp. 91-99.

Bandura, A. (1963) *Social learning and personality development*. New York: Holt, Rinehart, and Winston.

Barnes, C. (2015) 'The ideal work schedule as determined by circadian rhythms', *Harvard Business Review*. Available at: hbr.org/2015/01/the-ideal-work-schedule-as-determined-by-circadian-rhythms.

Barnes, R. (2015) *Information about ECT (Electro-convulsive therapy)*. Available at: www.rcpsych.ac.uk/healthadvice/treatmentswellbeing/ect.aspx (Accessed 21st August 2017).

Belbin, M. (1981) *Management teams*. London: Heinemann.

Berne, E. (1978) *Games people play: the psychology of human relations*. New York, NY: Grove Press.

Bowlby, J. (1951) *Maternal care and mental health*. Geneva, Switzerland: World Health Organisation.

Branstrom, R., Duncan, L. G. and Moskowitz, J. T. (2011) 'The association between dispositional mindfulness, psychological well-being, and perceived health in a Swedish population-based sample', *British Journal of Health Psychology* 16 (2) pp. 300-316.

Brontë, C. (1847) *Jane Eyre*. London: Smith, Elder & Co.

Brown, D. (2006) *The Heist*. Channel 4 [DVD].

Bryck, A. and Schneider, B. (2002) *Trust in schools: a core resource for improvement.* New York, NY: Russell Sage Foundation.

Callaghan, J. (2010) *A rational debate on the facts.* Available at: www.educationengland.org.uk/documents/speeches/1976ruskin.html (Accessed 17th June 2017).

Carroll, L. (2014) *Alice's adventures in Wonderland.* London: Macmillan Children's Classics.

Cherniss, C. and Goleman, D. (eds) (2001) *The emotionally intelligent work place.* San Francisco, CA: Jossey-Bass.

Choi, C. (2007) 'Strange but true: when half a brain is better than a whole one', *Scientific American.* Available at: www.scientificamerican.com/article/strange-but-true-when-half-brain-better-than-whole/.

Cloud, H. and Townsend, J. (1995) *Safe people.* Grand Rapids, MI: Zondervan.

Coates, M. (2008) *The constant leader.* London: Network Continuum.

Collison, C. and Parcell, G. (2001) *Learning to fly.* Chichester: Capstone Publishing Ltd.

Comer, J. P., Haynes, N. M., Joyner, E. T. and Ben-Avie, M. (1996) *Rallying the whole village: the Comer process for reforming education.* New York, NY: Teachers College Press.

Covey, S. R. (1989) *The 7 habits of highly effective people.* London: Simon and Schuster.

Craft, L. and Perna, F. (2004) 'The benefits of exercise for the clinically depressed', *Primary Care Companion to The Journal of Clinical Psychiatry* 6 (3) pp. 104-111.

Craig, G. (~1990) *EFT Manual.* Available at: eftmanual.weebly.com/uploads/3/1/0/1/3101311/eft_manual_6th_ed..pdf (Accessed 30th August 2017).

Crainer, S. and Dearlove, D. (2008) *The future of leadership.* Nottingham: NCSL.

Crockett, M. J., Siegel, J. Z., Kurth-Nelson, Z., Ousdal, O. T., Story, G., Frieband, C., Grosse-Rueskamp, J. M., Dayan, P. and Dolan, R. J. (2015) 'Dissociable effects of serotonin and dopamine on the valuation of harm in moral decision making', *Current Biology* 25 (14) pp. 1852-1859.

Csikszentmihalyi, M. (1990). *Flow: the psychology of optimal experience.* New York, NY: Harper & Row.

Csikszentmihalyi, M. (1997). *Finding flow: the psychology of engagement with everyday life.* New York, NY: Basic Books.

Curtis, R. and Elton, B. (1987) 'Nob and Nobility', *Blackadder the Third.* BBC.

Damassio, A. (1994) *Descartes' error: emotion, reason, and the human brain.* New York, NY: Putnam.

Danziger, S., Levav, J. and Avnaim-Pesso, L. (2011) 'Extraneous factors in judicial decisions', *PNAS* 108 (17) pp. 6889-6892.

Darley, J. and Batson, C. D. (1973) '"From Jerusalem to Jericho": a study of situational and dispositional variables in helping behavior', *Journal of Personality and Social Psychology* 27 (1) pp. 100-108.

Davies, R. (2017) 'Fixed-odds betting terminal review delayed until autumn', The Guardian, 30th June. Available at: www.theguardian.com/society/2017/jun/30/fixed-odds-betting-terminal-review-delayed-until-autumn

Day, C., Edwards, A., Griffiths, A. and Gu, Q. (2011) *Beyond survival: teachers and resilience.* Nottingham: University of Nottingham. Available at: www.nottingham.ac.uk/research/groups/crelm/documents/teachers-resilience/teachers-resilience.pdf

Denning, S. (2011) *The leader's guide to storytelling.* San Francisco, CA: Jossey-Bass.

Dijk, D., Groeger, J. A., Stanley, N. and Deacon, S. (2010) 'Age-related reduction in daytime sleep propensity and nocturnal slow wave sleep', *Sleep* 33 (2) pp. 211-223.

Dijk, D. and Winsky-Sommerer, R. (2012) 'Sleep', *New Scientist* 213 (2850).

Donnelly, L. (2017) 'One in three sick notes are for mental health problems, "alarming" report shows', *The Telegraph*, 31st August. Available at: www.telegraph.co.uk/news/2017/08/31/one-three-sick-notes-mental-health-problems-alarming-report/

Dunbar, R. (1998) *Grooming, gossip and the evolution of language.* Cambridge, MA: Harvard University Press.

Earley, P., Nelson, R., Higham, R., Bubb, S., Porritt, V., Coates, M. (2011) *Experiences of new headteachers in cities.* Nottingham: NCSL.

Eccles, J. (1996) *The brain and the unity of conscious experience.* Cambridge: Cambridge University Press.

Elliott, R. and Tyrell, M. (2002) *The depression learning path.* Oban: Uncommon Knowledge.

Epstein, S (1998) *Constructive thinking: the key to emotional intelligence.* Westport, CT: Praeger.

Everard, K. and Morris, G. (1996) *Effective school management.* London: Paul Chapman Publishing.

Evrad, H. C., Forro, T. and Logothetis, N. K. (2012) 'Von Economo neurons in the anterior insula of the macaque monkey', *Neuron* 74 (3) pp. 482-489.

Feder, A., Southwick, S. M., Goetz, R. R., Wang, Y., Alonso, A., Smith, B. W., Buchholz, K. R., Waldeck, T., Ameli, R., Moore, J., Hain, R., Charney, D. S. and Vythilingam, M. (2008) 'Posttraumatic growth in former Vietnam prisoners of war', *Psychiatry: Interpersonal & Biological Processes* 71 (4) pp. 359-370.

Flintham, A. (2003a) *Reservoirs of hope.* Nottingham, NCSL.

Flintham, A. (2003b) *When reservoirs run dry: why some headteachers leave headship early.* Nottingham, NCSL.

Forrest, L. (2008) 'The three faces of victim – an overview of the drama triangle', *lynneforrest. com.* Available at: www.lynneforrest.com/articles/2008/06/the-faces-of-victim/ (Accessed 26th July 2017).

Fotalia, L. (2017) 'The mere presence of your smartphone reduces brain power, study shows', *Science Daily.* Available at: www.sciencedaily.com/releases/2017/06/170623133039.htm (Accessed 5th September 2017).

Frey, C. and Osborne, M. A. (2013) *The* future *of employment: how susceptible are jobs to computerisation?* Oxford: Oxford University Press.

Frozen (2013) Directed by Chris Buck [Film]. Burbank, CA: Walt Disney Studios Motion Pictures.

Gallwey, T. (1974) *The inner game of tennis.* New York, NY: Bantam Books.

Gardner, H., De La Croix, H. and Tansey, R. G. (1970). *Art through the ages.* New York, NY: Harcourt, Brace and World.

George, B. (2003). *Authentic leadership: Rediscovering the secrets to creating lasting value.* San Francisco, CA: Jossey-Bass.

Gibbs, S. (2014) 'Elon Musk: artificial intelligence is our biggest existential threat', *The Guardian*, 27th October. Available at: www.theguardian.com/technology/2014/oct/27/elon-musk-artificial-intelligence-ai-biggest-existential-threat (Accessed 15th October 2017).

Giuliani, R. (2002) *Leadership.* London: Little, Brown Book Group.

Goel, A. (2016) *A teaching assistant called Jill Watson* [TED Talk]. Available at: www.youtube.com/watch?v=WbCguICyfTA (Accessed 18th October 2017).

Goleman, D. (1996) *Emotional intelligence: why it can matter more than IQ.* London: Bloomsbury.

Goleman, D. (1998) *Working with emotional intelligence.* London: Bloomsbury.

Goleman, D. (2001) 'An EI-based theory of performance' in Cherniss, C. and Goleman, D. (eds) *The emotionally intelligent workplace.* San Francisco, CA: Jossey-Bass, pp. 27-44.

Goleman, D., Boyatzis, R. and McKee, A. (2002) *The new leaders: transforming the art of leadership into the science of results.* London: Little, Brown Book Group.

Goleman, D. (2006) *Social intelligence: the new science of human relationships.* London: Hutchinson.

Goleman, D. (2008) 'When Emotional Intelligence does not matter more than IQ', *danielgoleman. info.* Available at: www.danielgoleman.info/when-emotional-intelligence-does-not-matter-more-than-iq/ (Accessed 14th May 2017).

Goodall, J (2017) 'Chimps as pets: the reality', *janegoodall.org.uk.* Available at: www.janegoodall.org.uk/chimpanzees/chimpanzee-central/15-chimpanzees/chimpanzee-central/28-chimps-as-pets-the-reality (Accessed 6th July 2017).

Grace, K., Salvatier, J., Dafoe, A., Zhang, B. and Evans, O. (2017) *When will AI exceed human performance?.* Available at: arxiv.org/pdf/1705.08807.pdf.

Griffin, J., Tyrrell, I. (2003) *The human givens: a new approach to emotional health and clear thinking.* Chalvington: Human Givens Publishing Ltd.

Griffin, J. and Tyrrell, I. (2014a) *How to lift depression...fast.* Chalvington: Human Givens Publishing Ltd.

Griffin, J. and Tyrrell, I. (2014b) *Why we dream: the definitive answer.* Chalvington: Human Givens Publishing Ltd.

Groysberg, B. and Slind, G. (2012) 'Leadership is a conversation', *Harvard Business Review*. Available at: hbr.org/2012/06/leadership-is-a-conversation.

The Guardian (2017a) 'Chilcot: Tony Blair was not "straight with the nation" over Iraq war', 6th July. Available at: www.theguardian.com/politics/2017/jul/06/chilcot-tony-blair-was-not-straight-with-the-nation-over-iraq-war (Accessed 6th July 2017).

The Guardian (2017b) 'The *Guardian* view on betting terminals: an outrageous racket', 20th August. Available at: www.theguardian.com/commentisfree/2017/aug/20/the-guardian-view-on-betting-terminals-an-outrageous-racket.

Gunia, B. C., Barnes, C. M. and Sah, S. (2014) 'The morality of larks and owls: unethical behavior depends on chronotype as well as time of day', *Psychological Science* 25 (12) pp. 2272–2274.

Heifetz, R., Grashow, A. and Linsky, M. (2009) *The practice of adaptive leadership: tools and tactics for changing your organization and the world.* Boston, MA: Harvard Business Review Press.

Heinlein, R. (1953) *Assignment in eternity.* Reading, PA: Fantasy Press

Hitchcock, A. (2016) *Reform report.* Available at: www.reform.co.uk/publications/nhs_reform (Accessed 15th October 2017).

Hofstede, G. (1984) 'The cultural relativity of the quality of life concept', *Academy of Management Review* 9 (3) pp. 389-398.

Hopkins, D. (2007) *Every school a great school: realizing the potential of system leadership.* Maidenhead: Open University Press.

Hugo, V. (2002) *Les misérables.* Ware: Wordsworth Classics.

Hurley, T. and Brown, J. (2009) 'Conversational leadership, thinking together for a change', *Systems Thinker* 20 (9) Available at: thesystemsthinker.com/conversational-leadership-thinking-together-for-a-change/.

Jarvis, D. (2017) 'Stressed teachers offered electric shock therapy to combat anxiety and depression', *The Telegraph*, 1st July. Available at: www.telegraph.co.uk/education/2017/07/01/stressed-teachers-offered-electric-shock-therapy-combat-anxiety/ (Accessed 21st August 2017).

Jumanji (1995) Directed by Joe Johnston [Film]. Culver City, CA: TriStar Pictures.

Junger, S. (1997) *The perfect storm: a true story of men against the sea.* Hammersmith: Harper Collins.

Karpman, S. (1972) *Eric Berne memorial scientific award lecture.* Available at: www.karpmandramatriangle.com/pdf/AwardSpeech.pdf (Accessed 26th July 2017).

Kelltrill (2015) 'The problems with insights discovery personality assessments', *Waxing Apocalyptic blog.* Available at: waxingapocalyptic.com/2015/10/23/the-problems-with-insights-discovery-personality-assessments/ (Accessed 10th July 2017).

King, L. A., King, D. W., Fairbank, J. A., Keane, T. M. and Adams, G. A. (1998) 'Resilience-recovery factors in posttraumatic stress disorder among female and male Vietnam veterans: hardiness, postwar social support, and additional stressful life events', *Journal of Personality and Social Psychology* 74 (2) pp. 420–434.

Kolb, D. A. (1984) *Experiential learning*. Englewood Cliffs, NJ: Prentice Hall.

Kouchaki, M. and Smith, I. H. (2014) 'The morning morality effect: the influence of time of day on unethical behavior', *Psychological Science* 25 (1) pp. 95-102.

Kustenmacher, T. (2004) *How to simplify your life*. New York, NY: McGraw-Hill.

Lencioni, P. (2002) *The five dysfunctions of a team*. San Francisco, CA: Jossey-Bass.

Levitin, D. J. (2015) 'Why the modern world is bad for your brain', *The Guardian*, 18th January. Available at: www.theguardian.com/science/2015/jan/18/modern-world-bad-for-brain-daniel-j-levitin-organized-mind-information-overload.

Liao, S. (2017) 'A five-minute meditation' in Gibbs, N. (ed.) *Mindfulness, a pathway to health and happiness*. New York, NY: Time Books.

Loftus, E. F. and Palmer, J. C. (1974) 'Reconstruction of automobile destruction: an example of the interaction between language and memory', *Journal of Verbal Learning and Verbal Behavior* 13 (5) pp. 585-589.

Lord, C., Ross, L. and Lepper, M. (1979) 'Biased assimilation and attitude polarization: the effects of prior theories on subsequently considered evidence', *Journal of Personality and Social Psychology* 37 (11) pp. 2098-2109.

Louis, K. S. and Kruse, S. D. (eds) (1995) *Professionalism and community: perspectives on reforming urban schools*. Thousand Oaks, CA: Corwin Press.

Luders, E., Kurth, F., Mayer, E. A., Toga, A. W., Narr, K. L. and Gaser, C. (2012) 'The unique brain anatomy of meditation practitioners: alterations in cortical gyrification', *Frontiers in Human Neuroscience* 6 (34)

Machiavelli, N. (1985) *The Prince*. Mansfield, H. (trans.) Chicago, IL: University of Chicago Press

Macoby, M. (2001) 'Narcissistic leaders: the incredible pros, the inevitable cons', *Harvard Business Review*. Available at: hbr.org/2004/01/narcissistic-leaders-the-incredible-pros-the-inevitable-cons.

Male, T., Greany, T. and Coates, M. (2017) *Leadership in multi-academy trusts*. London: UCL Institute of Education.

Mansell, W. (2015) 'School whistleblowers call for naming and shaming', *The Guardian*, 13th January. Available at: www.theguardian.com/education/2015/jan/13/school-coursework-cheat-whistleblowers.

Maslow, A. (1943) 'A theory of human motivation', *Psychological Review* 50 (4) pp. 370–96.

McKie, R. (2006) *Face of Britain*. London: Simon and Schuster.

Megginson, D. and Clutterbuck, D. (2012) *Techniques for coaching and mentoring*. London: Routledge.

Mehrabian, A. and Wiener, M. (1967) 'Decoding of inconsistent communications', *Journal of Personality and Social Psychology* 6 (1) pp. 109-114.

Meier, D. (1995) *The power of their ideas: lessons for America from a small school in Harlem*. Boston, MA: Beacon Press.

Milgram, S. (1963) 'Behavioral Study of Obedience', *Journal of Abnormal and Social Psychology* 67 (4) pp. 371-378.

Miller, E. (2013) Digital *lives – the science behind multitasking* [Video]. Available at: www.youtube. com/watch?v=E5JNpTySQ_8&t=13s (Accessed 5th September 2017).

Mueller, P. and Oppenheimer, D. (2014) 'The pen is mightier than the keyboard', *Psychological Science* 25 (6) pp. 1159-1168.

NASUWT (2016) *Big Question Survey Report 2016*. Birmingham: NASUWT.

NHS (2017) 'Mindfulness', *NHS Choices*. Available at: www.nhs.uk/Conditions/stress-anxiety-depression/pages/mindfulness.aspx) (Accessed 1st September 2017).

Nisbett, R. E. and Wilson, T. D. (1977) 'Telling more than we can know: verbal reports on mental processes', *Psychological Review* 84 (3) pp. 231-259.

Nixon, P. G. (1976) 'The human function curve', *Practitioner* 217 (1301) pp. 765-770.

The Observer Magazine (2004) 'What's the word?', 8th February.

Ochsner, K. N., Ray, R. D., Cooper, J. C., Robertson, E. R., Chopra, S., Gabrieli, J. D. and Gross, J. J. (2004). 'For better or for worse: neural systems supporting the cognitive down- and up-regulation of negative emotion', *Neuroimage* 23 (2) pp. 483-499.

O'Connor, J. and Lages, A. (2007) *How coaching works: the essential guide to the history and practice of effective coaching*. London: A & C Black.

Osborne, H. (2014) 'Psychometric tests in job interviews: what are they looking for?', *The Guardian*, 29th January. Available at: www.theguardian.com/money/shortcuts/2014/jan/29/psychometric-tests-job-interviews-what-for (Accessed 1st August 2017).

Ozimek, A. (2016) 'The Great Man Theory of Trump', *Forbes*, 31st January. Available at: www.forbes.com/sites/modeledbehavior/2016/01/31/great-man-trump/#7b7a232c486b (Assessed 8th July 2017).

Panayotis, P. (2017) 'Non-prescription use of Ritalin linked to adverse side effects', *buffalo.edu*. Buffalo, NY: University of Buffalo. Available at: www.buffalo.edu/news/releases/2017/05/007.html (Accessed 16th September 2017).

Parr, L. A., Waller, B. M. and Fugate, J. (2005) 'Emotional communication in primates: implications for neurobiology', *Current Opinion in Neurobiology* 15 (6) pp. 716-720.

Pask, R. and Joy, B. (2007) *Mentoring-coaching: a guide for education professionals*. Maidenhead: Open University Press.

Paton, G. (2014) 'School introduces "no mornings" policy for tired teenagers', *The Telegraph*, 9th May. Available at: www.telegraph.co.uk/education/educationnews/10818678/School-introduces-no-mornings-policy-for-tired-teenagers.html (Accessed 1st December 2016).

Paxton, J. M., Ungar, L. and Greene, J. D. (2012) 'Reflection and reasoning in moral judgment', *Cognitive Science* 36 (1) pp. 163-177.

Peck, S. (1988) *People of the lie*. London: Arrow Books.

Perry, G. (2012) *Behind the shock machine: the untold story of the notorious Milgram psychology experiments*. New York, NY: The New Press.

Peters, S. (2012) *The chimp paradox*. London: Ebury Publishing.

Pizarro, D. A., Inbar, Y. and Helion, C. (2011) 'On disgust and moral judgement', *Emotion Review 3 (3) pp. 267-268*.

Pizarro, D. A. (2013) *The strange politics of disgust* [TED Talk]. Available at: www.youtube.com/watch?v=5YL3LT1ZvOM (Accessed 26th March 2017).

Raiders of the lost ark (1981) Directed by Steven Spielberg [Film]. Hollywood, CA: Paramount.

Ramachandran, V. S. (2012) *The tell-tale brain: a neuroscientist's quest for what makes us human*. London: Windmill Books.

The Revenant (2015) Directed by Alejandro G. Inarritu [Film]. Los Angeles, CA: 20th Century Fox.

Riley, K. (2013) *Leadership of place: stories for schools in the US, UK and South Africa*. London: Bloomsbury.

Riley, K. (2017) *Place, belonging and school leadership*. London: Bloomsbury.

Riley, K., Coates, M. and Perez Martinez, S. (2017) *Place and belonging in schools: unlocking possibilities*. London: UCL Institute of Education.

Ritchie, M. (2013) '24-hour study people? Why I take Ritalin', *Channel 4 News*. Available at: www.channel4.com/news/ritalin-rise-adhd-uk-student-focus-silk-road-secret-web (Accessed 16th September 2017).

Rittel, H. W. J. and Webber, M. M. (1973) 'Dilemmas in a general theory of planning', *Policy Sciences 4 (2) pp. 155-169*.

Robotham, D., Chakkalackal, L. and Cyhlarova, E. (2011) *The impact of sleep on health and wellbeing*. London: Mental Health Foundation.

Rogers, J. (2012) *Coaching skills: a handbook*. Maidenhead: Open University Press.

Rottenberg, J. (2014) *The depths: the evolutionary origins of the depression epidemic*. New York, NY: Basic Books.

Rushdie, S. (1988) *The Satanic verses*. London: Penguin Random House.

Sage, R. (2000) *Class talk*. London: Network Continuum.

Sage, R. (2017) 'The educational context' in Sage, R. (ed.) *Paradoxes in education*. Rotterdam, The Netherlands: Sense Publishers.

Sale, J. (2007) *Motivational maps*. Bournemouth: Motivational Maps.

Sale, J. (2016) *Mapping motivation: unlocking the key to employee energy and engagement*. Abingdon: Routledge.

Salzberg, S. (2010) *Real happiness: the power of meditation*. New York, NY: Workman.

Savage, A. (2006) *Slow leadership: civilising the organization*. Australia: Pusch Ridge Publishing.

Schein, E. (2004) *Organizational culture and leadership.* San Francisco, CA: Jossey-Bass.

Schein, E. (2008) 'Creating and managing a learning culture' in Gallos, J. (ed.) *Business leadership.* San Francisco, CA: Jossey-Bass.

Schein, E. (2010) *Organizational culture and leadership.* San Francisco, CA: Jossey-Bass.

Scott, S. (2002) *Fierce conversations: achieving success in work and in life, one conversation at a time.* London: Piatkus.

Scott, S. (2009) *Fierce leadership: a bold alternative to the worst 'best' practices of business today.* New York, NY: Crown Business.

Seligman, M. (1972) 'Learned helplessness', *Annual Review of Medicine* 23 (1) pp. 407-412.

Seligman, M. (1975) *Helplessness: on depression, development, and death.* San Francisco, CA: W. H. Freeman.

Seligman, M. (1988) 'People born after 1945 were ten times more likely to suffer from depression than people born 50 years earlier' in Buie, J. (ed.) *'Me' decades generate depression: individualism erodes commitment to others.* Washington, DC: APA Monitor.

Seligman, M. (2008) *The new era of positive psychology* [TED Talk]. Available at: www.youtube.com/watch?v=9FBxfd7DL3E (Accessed 10th August 2017).

Selye, H. (1956) *The stress of life.* New York, NY: McGraw-Hill.

Senge, P. (1992) *The fifth discipline.* London: Century Business.

Shaw, G. B. (1916) *Pygmalion.* New York, NY: Brentano.

Shaw, R. B. (1997) *Trust in the balance: building successful organizations on results, integrity and concern.* San Francisco, CA: Jossey-Bass.

Sills, J. (2013) 'The power of no', *Psychology today.* Available at: www.psychologytoday.com/articles/201311/the-power-no (Accessed 5th May 2013).

Simon, P. and Garfunkel, A. (1966) '59th Street Bridge Song', *Parsley, sage, rosemary and thyme.* New York, NY: Columbia Records.

Sleepio (2012) *The Great British sleep survey: new data on the impact of poor sleep.* Available at: www.greatbritishsleepsurvey.com/ (Accessed 23rd August 2017).

Solms, M. (2000) 'Dreaming and REM sleep are controlled by different brain mechanisms', *Behavioral and Brain Sciences* 23 (6) pp. 843-850.

Southwick and Charney (2013) 'Ready for anything', *Scientific American Mind* 24 (3) pp. 32-41.

Speirs, R. (2016) *The art of international school headship.* Market Harborough: RSAcademics.

Ter Horst, G. (ed.) (1999) *The nervous system and the heart.* New York, NY: Humana Press.

Thomas, W. (2016) *Soul candy.* Stroud: Chrysalis Poetry.

Toffler, A. (1970) *Future shock.* London: The Bodley Head.

Tschannen-Moran, M., and Hoy, W. K. (2000) 'A multidisciplinary analysis of the nature, meaning, and measurement of trust', *Review of Educational Research* 70 (4) pp. 547-593.

Tyrrell, I. and Griffin, J. (2013) *Human givens: the new approach to emotional health.* Chalvington: Human Givens Publishing.

Tyrrell, M. (2007) *Emotional trance states.* Oban: Uncommon Knowledge.

Tyrrell, M. (2013) *How well do you know yourself?* Oban: Uncommon Knowledge.

Tyrrell, M. (2015) *Uncommon psychotherapy.* Oban: Uncommon Knowledge.

University of Worcester (2016) *Learning journals.* Available at: www.worcester.ac.uk/studyskills/documents/Learning_Journals_2016.pdf (Accessed 24/3/2017).

Vederese, M. and Roth, H. (2011) 'Kekule's dream', *Chemdoodle.* Available at: web.chemdoodle.com/kekules-dream/.

Veenman, D. and Hart, G. (2014) *The rise of 'conversational leadership',* London: The Right Conversation Limited.

Vodicka, D. (2006) The four elements of trust. *Principal Leadership (Middle School ed.)* 7 (3) pp. 27-30.

Von Radowitz, J. (2017) 'Intelligent machines will replace teachers within 10 years, leading public school headteacher predicts', *The Independent,* 11th September. Available at: www.independent.co.uk/news/education/education-news/intelligent-machines-replace-teachers-classroom-10-years-ai-robots-sir-anthony-sheldon-wellington-a7939931.html (Accessed 15th October 2017).

Ward, A., Duke, K., Gneezy, A. and Bos, M. (2017) 'Brain drain: the mere presence of one's own smartphone reduces available cognitive capacity', *Journal of the Association for Consumer Research* 2 (2) pp. 140-154.

Weil, A. (2015) *Asleep in 60 seconds* [Video]. Available at: www.youtube.com/watch?v=gz4G31LGyog (Accessed 30th August 2017).

Wells, M. (2014) *Courage and air warfare: the allied aircrew experience in the second world war.* London: Routledge.

West-Burnham, J. and Coates, M. (2005) *Personalised education – transforming education.* Stafford: Network Educational Press.

West-Burnham, J. and Coates, M. (2006) *Personalizing learning: transforming education for every child, a practical handbook.* Stafford: Network Educational Press.

Westen, D., Blagov, S., Harenski, K., Kilts, C. and Hamann, S. (2006) 'Neural bases of motivated reasoning: an FMRI study of emotional constraints on partisan political judgment in the 2004 US presidential election', *Journal of Cognitive Neuroscience* 18 (11) pp. 1947-1958.

Whitmore, J. (1992) *Coaching for performance.* London: Nicholas Breasley.

Wilson, H. (1963) *Labour's plan for science.* London: Labour Party.

Zeidner, M., Roberts, R. and Matthews, G. (2002) 'Can emotional intelligence be schooled? A critical review', *Educational Psychologist* 37 (4) pp. 215-231.